THE BATTLE HARDENED DEVELOPER

How to identify your enemy, find your allies, and prevail over your inner saboteur

1st Edition

Fiodar Sazanavets

Simple Programmer LLC

Copyright © 2022 by Simple Programmer LLC.

Publisher: John Z. Sonmez
Project Manager: Robin de Jongh
Development Editor: Jo Finchen-Parsons
Cover designer: Bogdan Matei

TABLE OF CONTENTS

PROLOGUE

These days, programming is no longer seen as a profession for socially awkward nerds. The career is now generally accepted as prestigious, as it pays really well. Many people dream of having a successful career in IT. But of those who try, many hit the ceiling in their career really quick. Many even struggle to get started.

If you are one of such people and you feel like you got stuck in your IT career, then you need to understand that it's not all your fault. There is a war going on against you. The biggest reason why people get stuck in their IT career is because such a career requires a good ability to focus. But there are so many distractions around you these days, that it's sometimes extremely hard to focus. And all of this is by design rather than by accident.

There are many companies who want to take all your attention from you. Your attention is being converted into their profits. But since your attention is a finite resource, you won't have much left of it to focus on your productive work. And this is why many IT professionals hit the ceiling in their career beyond which they can't progress.

But the good news is that you can win this war. You can fight off all of the distractions and become a disciplined and productive software developer that everyone will want to hire. And this book will teach you how.

My name is Fiodar Sazanavets. I have made a successful career in software engineering. In less than a decade, I worked my way up to a position of lead software engineer at a reputable company located in London. I am also an author of various online courses on programming. There are certain areas of software engineering that I have mastered to an extent that I use them almost intuitively. My expertise in those areas is not only recognized by my employer, but also by various organizations that publish educational material on programming. I get approached by these organizations on a regular basis and I get asked to create content for their platforms.

But at one point in my life, programming was something that I thought to be too hard for me to do. Even though I always liked computers, even since I was a kid, the art of programming always looked like black magic to me. I always assumed that only the smartest of us ever get a chance to become truly successful in the programming profession.

This is why, when it was time for me to go to university, I didn't even choose to study anything related to programming. I have chosen environmental biology instead. And then, when I had successfully completed my course, I stayed on to do a masters degree, which was in a subject related to environmental science. I have started learning how to code only after I've completed my masters degree. And this was purely out of necessity.

I have managed to get a job after I've graduated and my job was directly related to what I've studied. I was a flood risk analyst and I loved what I did. Plus, it felt good to know that you actually do something that would benefit the society. But there was only one major problem with this type of career: the salary.

My position paid less than what a warehouse operator at my local supermarket was earning. Initially, I thought that this was because I was fresh out of university. But then I found out that even the senior flood risk analysts were paid badly. For example, one of my senior colleagues was driving a very old car with a leaking sunroof and regularly complained about how bad his salary was.

This is when I realized that flood risk analyst would not be my job forever. I had some reasonably big life goals and my salary wasn't sufficient to achieve any of them. Yes, I was helping people not to get their houses flooded. But I also realized that the majority of people who benefited from my work were homeowners, while, with my salary, there was absolutely no chance that I would ever become a home owner myself. So I needed to change my career and I needed to do it as soon as possible.

Going back to university to study something else was out of the question. It took too long and I didn't want to get into even more student debt. I needed to change my profession to something that I could learn quickly and at as little financial cost as possible. And, after doing some research, I found that programming was such a thing. There were plenty of testimonies online made by self-taught programmers who were earning six-figure salaries. So, despite my fear of programming, I decided to give it a go.

Even though it was scary, it still felt better than my current situation was at the time. And this was what motivated me to spend pretty much all of my free time learning how to code by brute-forcing my way through difficult programming concepts.

I eventually managed to learn enough to become a junior developer. And as soon as I felt ready, I changed my job. I now was a full-time programmer. I was over the moon at first, but then just settled into a comfortable routine. And this is when my progress began to stagnate.

I could no longer motivate myself to spend my free time sharpening my skills. I was just doing the absolute minimum my employer required me to do. And even that was hard sometimes. I had real trouble focusing.

I still really wanted to be successful in my software development career. During my initial learning phase, I fell in love with programming, so it was a job I wanted to do more than anything else. But when I actually needed to get some programming done, getting started was a real chore. There were so many other fun things I wanted to do instead of programming. And I would often just succumb to the urge to procrastinate, because fighting the urge was so hard.

This is when I started seeing all of this as a battle. To me, this was an easy analogy to make, as I have always been interested in warfare and martial arts. I have even thought of joining the armed forces at one point in my life. And this metaphor proved itself to be effective. With its help, I was able to make myself productive once again, which has helped me to progress my career.

As this was now a battle, I started looking for the enemy. I started studying what makes us want to procrastinate and how to fight it. And, because I came from a science background and already had some knowledge of how the brain works from my biology degree, the science behind procrastination is what I started studying first.

Soon, it became clear to me why our brain wants us to procrastinate. I tried and tested various techniques of tricking the brain to focus instead of urging me to succumb to distractions. Some of these techniques were more effective than others. But there were some that truly stood out in their effectiveness. I was also able to modify some of the well-known techniques to suit me personally.

When I started practicing these techniques, my progress in my career went up again. I became way more efficient in my work than I ever was before. The quality of my work went up. And I was able to reach the level of a senior software developer in less than five years, which is a good result for someone who was completely self-taught as a programmer.

I have been using these techniques since then and they have never failed me. When needed, I can obtain a state of deep focus and completely forget about any distractions. I want as many current or aspiring software developers as possible to know these techniques too. And this is why I wrote this book.

But it's not merely about the techniques. Some mindset changes have also helped me achieve success in my career. In a way, I needed to become a different person from who I was when I was going through the motions, doing bare minimum and procrastinating a lot. But luckily, I found some ways of building the right type of mindset for becoming a person I wanted to be. And this is what I also want to share with you.

In this book, I provide distilled information on what you would need to do to have a successful programming career. The book only contains recommendations that I personally tried, tested, and found to be effective.

We will begin with covering some science behind procrastination and focus. As someone who came from a science background, I found that techniques work more effectively if you understand why they work. And this is why I thought that putting basic science into the book was necessary. But don't worry, we won't go too deep into the science of the brain. After all, this is not a book on neuroscience or psychology. We will cover just enough that you will understand how various businesses, such as social media companies, hijack the workings of your brain for their own profit.

You will learn why your brain wants to follow the path of least resistance, which helps these companies to appropriate your attention without you realizing it. But you will also learn how your habits form, so you can fight effectively against all of the distractions that are being sent your way.

Then we will move on to the ways you can modify your core beliefs, so they would be fully in-line with what you would want to achieve in your career. You will find out why it's important to surround yourself with successful programmers. Some of the other attitude-building techniques we will talk about are fairly obvious, like accepting ownership for everything that happens in your environment. But we will also talk about things that are much less intuitive, despite being very effective. For example, you will discover what IT professionals can learn from monks.

Finally, we will cover the actual tricks that you can implement in your work to make the process of maintaining focus much easier. If you regularly visit programming productivity forums, you might have heard about some of them already, such as Pomodoro technique or pre-planning your work. But there are also some tricks that aren't very well-known in the IT industry. One of them is Shisa Kanko, which was originally developed to help Japanese railway workers to maintain focus. But it appears that it can be used just as effectively to help programmers maintain their focus too.

After reading this book, your programming career will never be the same again. Your output will improve in terms of both the quality and the quantity. This will not go unnoticed by your clients, bosses, and co-workers. But perhaps more importantly, this book will help you to enjoy your programming career much more.

CHAPTER 1

WHY SOCIAL MEDIA IS YOUR MAIN ENEMY

The tycoons of social media have to stop pretending that they're friendly nerd gods building a better world and admit they're just tobacco farmers in T-shirts selling an addictive product to children. Because, let's face it, checking your "likes" is the new smoking.

—Cal Newport

Every programmer knows what skills they need to master to be fully competent. If you know a number of programming languages well and know how to build good-quality software from scratch - then you can call yourself a professional programmer.

But these skills are not sufficient for you to become a truly great programmer. If you merely know how to code, you will be merely average. You will have to deal with a lot of competition from other programmers and your salary, while probably being higher than average, would still be much lower than what it could have been. Plus, if you merely meet minimum criteria for being a professional software developer, it would be next to impossible for you to get into one of the FAANG companies (Facebook, Amazon, Apple, Netflix, Google). You need to truly stand out to be a member of the elite software development club.

Have you ever wondered what makes famous software engineers, the truly elite, like Kent Beck, Scott Hanselman, Robert C. Martin (who is also known as Uncle Bob) and Martin Fowler so successful and so different from most of your colleagues? It may, at first, seem that those people are geniuses and that you have to be born special to achieve their level. But it's not necessarily the case.

If you look at what these people do and how they do it, it becomes apparent that their main skills aren't the hard technical skills. And it's not even the so-called soft skills. It's something way more fundamental that makes them as exceptional as they are.

It doesn't matter that much how many languages and best practices you know. What those exceptional soft engineers know is that developing meta-skills matters way more. Meta-skills is an all-encompassing term that refers to components of your personality that you can consciously develop, such as habits, routines, self-awareness and general mindset, etc..

In this book, you will learn a whole range of meta-skills that, if incorporated into your daily routine, will help you to become a programmer that truly stands out from the crowd. You will be able to master anything much quicker than most people. Your competition will be substantially reduced, companies will want to hire you and everybody will want to pay you well. Your job will become easier, more enjoyable and something you can switch-off from when the time is right. You'll be able to compartmentalize and improve your work–life balance.

But before you can learn what to do, you need to learn what you must stop doing. There is a hidden war going on and many developers are unaware of it. The enemy is cunning, because it presents itself as a friend. But the enemy is dangerous, as it can single-handedly render all of your hard work on your professional development null and void.

This enemy is social media. And you, as a programmer, are especially vulnerable to it.

Why social media is your most dangerous enemy

Social media is everywhere and it's extremely rare to find somebody who doesn't use it. And there is a good reason for this.

Since social media became popular, it became extremely easy to meet new people and keep in touch with old friends, regardless of where in the world they currently are. Also, never before it was so easy to share content that can be seen by literally millions of people across the globe.

There are indeed many great benefits that social media has brought to us. But it's not all as nice and rosy as it may seem at the first glance.

If you have been monitoring the tech industry for a while, you have probably seen various social media companies being involved in scandals on a regular basis. A lot of them are about privacy issues, tax avoidance and meddling with democratic elections.

But it's none of these issues that you need to worry about as someone who aspires to be an elite-level programmer. Taxes that big corporations do or don't pay don't affect your daily work life or your productivity. You are probably educated enough to spot manipulated news or content on your feed, or at least to do the research to make your own mind up during any elections that you choose to participate in. And you probably already understand the pros and cons of sharing your data on the web and what problems it has in terms of privacy.

But there is one problem with social media that you should definitely be concerned about. If you are ambitious and your goal is to become a master of your craft, nothing can derail your effort as much as social media. It can easily nullify all of your efforts to build good productivity habits. And it's the main enemy of deep work that we will discuss in **chapter 2.**

This is precisely why Cal Newport, the author of the Deep Work book, doesn't use it. And this is why he spoke against it at length in both Deep Work and his another bestselling title, Digital Minimalism. [1] In the latter book especially, he didn't pull any punches while talking about social media. This is what he said about it:

> *"The tycoons of social media have to stop pretending that they're friendly nerd gods building a better world and admit they're just tobacco farmers in T-shirts selling an addictive product to children. Because, let's face it, checking your "likes" is the new smoking."*

As someone who aspires to become a great software developer that everyone would want to hire, you must know that nothing can derail your effort as social media can. Seemingly benign platform where you have a laugh with your friends and share funny memes can actually substantially slow down, or even completely derail, your career.

Social media is the single most powerful thing that can prevent you from building the right habits. If not used with caution, it is something that can make deep work impossible.

And it's not an accident that social media is an extremely powerful distraction that can prevent you from building the right habits to become a top-notch software developer that everyone will want to hire. It's been deliberately designed this way.

What social media wants from you is not in your best interest

If you are a user of social media, you'll probably know how hard sometimes it can be to resist it.

Chances are, you have been in a situation where you have opened your Facebook or Twitter app just to check a couple of posts. Then, hours later, you realize that you have just wasted a lot of time scrolling the timeline and being engaged in pointless arguments with various people. It's like your conscious mind got completely switched off and autopilot mode kicked in.

Unfortunately, this is all by design. This sort of behavior is precisely what social media companies want from you. They want your attention and they want it undivided. They don't want anything else to compete with them for your attention.

Have you ever wondered why social media is generally free, even though you can do so many seemingly useful things on it? After all, a lot of time and effort has been spent designing all of these features that make social media so content-rich. And you probably know that it's all been made by people who are being paid extremely well for their jobs.

So, how can social media companies earn billions from a platform that is free to use, while also paying their developers king's ransom? Where's the catch, you may be wondering? Well, there is indeed a catch. And it's quite a serious one.

The thing that you should remember is that if something is free for you to use, then it's probably you who is actually the product. And this principle absolutely is the case with social media. It is a business, but you are not a customer of it. Advertisement agencies are.

Social media platforms, such as Facebook, Twitter and Instagram, are actually advertisement platforms. Businesses and other types of organizations pay money to those platforms to host their adverts hosted on them. And the platforms serve them in the best way they can.

Social media platforms already have a lot of your data. You have voluntarily given it all away. Not only have you put your personal details when you registered, but since then, you have also been giving a lot of unambiguous information about your personal preferences by interacting with the content on the platforms.

Everything that you do on social media is being traced. And this is how the algorithms know your likes and dislikes, your religious and political views, and more.

How corporations monetize your attention

For advertisers, it's a true goldmine of information. No longer people have to express their preferences in surveys. You don't have to rely on people to fill them truthfully or even fill them at all. You are constantly giving away all the truthful information voluntarily without even being aware of it. And it doesn't even have to be you actively expressing your opinion in posts or in comments. A lot about you can be said simply by checking what pages you like to visit and what type of content you like to view.

Once advertisers have this information, they will be able to decide which products and services you would most likely be interested in. And if you constantly see ads that have been specifically targeted at you, there is a much greater chance that you will actually end up buying something that you see in those ads. But even if you don't buy anything, the mere act of clicking on an ad earns money for those who run social media platforms.

For advertisers, this is perfect. Contextual advertisement based on a user's personal preferences is the most efficient form of advertisement that has ever existed.

For example, TV commercials are expensive. And it's always the same commercial that is being shown to absolutely everyone that is watching the same show on TV, despite the fact that the show will probably be watched by people whose interests vary widely.

With contextual advertising, it's all different. It's way cheaper for a business to host adverts on a social media platform, because they tend to get charged for the actual result (e.g. per every click). So, if only very few people have expressed any interest in a product, the business will be charged very little.

Also, the advert will only be shown to people who match the profile of a potential customer for that product or service. Analytical algorithms running in the background will determine suitable context for the advert and will insert it there.

Of course, they don't get it right all the time. Sometimes, you may see weirdly irrelevant products being advertised to you. But still, the chance that any given advert will be shown in the right context is quite high.

And this is why social media wants to monopolize your attention. The more time you spend on it - the more information you will give away about yourself and the more ads you will see. The more relevant ads you will see - the more of them you will click on. And those ads will then be better targeted.

This is why social media giants work tirelessly to ensure two things:

1. That you, as a user, willingly give away as much information about yourself as possible, so the ads are targeted better.

2. That you, as a user, spend as much time on the platform as possible, so you see as many ads as possible and click on as many of them as possible.

So, the social media will hire an army of experts of human behavior to ensure that these two goals are met. And, as the technologies evolve, so are the ways to manipulate you. [2]

It's a brilliant proposition for the advertisers. But it's not so brilliant for you. It's all done at the expense of your attention and your goals.

So no, social media is not there to enhance your life. On the contrary, it wants to take away as much of it as possible. And even though it doesn't ask you for money, it will probably get more than its fair share from the companies whose product you'll buy after seeing it on their platform.

Why social media is the main enemy of deep work

Your ability to do deep work is one of the most important meta-skills for a successful software development career. And it's even better if you can do it in the state of flow.

But the key element of deep work is that it implies that all of your attention is given to a complex task at hand. To get completely into the process and clear your brain of any distracting thoughts, it may take you some time. But social media is very good at ensuring that it never happens.

You might be familiar with a situation where you were trying to focus, but then you have received a notification on your smartphone. Suddenly, all the thoughts about the task you were trying to complete have evaporated. All you think of is what this notification is about.

Often, it will be something extremely trivial. For example, Facebook may notify you that someone you don't even know has posted in a group that you are a member of.

On the one hand, it will be easy just to disregard this notification and get back to your original task. But on the other hand, your thought process has already been interrupted. If you were in the state of flow, you aren't anymore. You've been yanked out of it. The damage has already been done. And now you have to start from square one.

But it's even worse if the notification was about something that's meaningful to you. If somebody liked your post, perhaps you want to see who that was. If somebody commented under your post or has replied to your comment, you would want to write something back.

And now you have completely forgotten about the task you were supposed to complete. All your brain power is being used on compiling a reply.

And it's not a big of a deal if it was a positive comment and you came back with a nice reply. You can still get back to your work. It's much worse if somebody has actually said something negative that has been addressed to you. In this case, you can try to get back to work, but your ability to focus will be close to zero. Instead of thinking about your task, you will be thinking about what was said and what to do next.

Even if you have successfully managed to get back to your task after spending a couple of minutes on social media, that's a context switch. And context switches deplete your mental energy. If you do too many of them within a short period of time, there won't be enough of it left to actually progress your task.

But sometimes you won't even instantly get back to your task after receiving a notification. Alongside the post that the notification related to you will see some other interesting content, like funny memes, a link to some news article or anything else that will attract your attention. And that where you can fall into an autopilot mode and start going deep down the rabbit hole.

Then you will just carry on scrolling down to see if there are any more interesting posts. But the posts will never end. No matter how far down you scroll, the content will keep appearing. And this is how you can waste several hours if you are not careful.

After a while, you may wake up from this semi-trance state and will realize that you still have an unfinished task to do. But after processing such a high quantity of extremely diverse information, doing meaningful work will probably be the last thing you will want to do. Instead, you will want to carry on procrastinating.

And no, I'm not just describing the behavior of someone who struggles to control their impulses. Most of you will recognise yourself in these examples. This is how pretty much any normal person will react to social media, unless they have been explicitly taught about its addictive qualities.

But even worse is the fact that you don't necessarily need a physical trigger to get distracted from your work by social media. Even if you have switched off all notifications on your smartphone, you may still get distracted. And there is an important reason for this.

If you have interacted with social media enough times, your brain will remember these interactions. And it will want to repeat them. So, an urge to check your Facebook may come simply as a thought in your head.

But what's so special about the interactions with social media that makes your brain want to repeat them? Well, there is nothing special per se. But the whole platform was deliberately designed in such a way that these interactions hijack the reward mechanism of your brain.

Almost anything you do on social media releases large quantities of dopamine. And that's precisely why social media is something you can get easily addicted to.

What is dopamine and how is it involved in addictions?

Dopamine is one of the main neurotransmitters in an animal brain. But the specific characteristic of dopamine is that it's the neurotransmitter of anticipation rather than pleasure.

And because it's the neurotransmitter of anticipation, it's not the process of getting an actual reward that triggers it. It gets triggered when you are close to getting a reward. [3]

This neurotransmitter is extremely useful from an evolutionary perspective. It's what drives animals to perform the actions that are likely to bring a reward to them. Essentially, this is the neurotransmitter that has been driving animals to survive.

When one of our ancestors was chasing an antelope, dopamine would kick in when the antelope was about to get caught. When our ancestors battled it out, it's the dopamine that motivated exhausted warriors to fight on when they were getting closer to victory.

Without dopamine, we would not have motivation to do anything. Brendon Burchard, a performance coach and New York Times bestselling author, said the following about dopamine:

> *"People say, "I wish I had more motivation today, because then*
> *I would try something." But our thinking is backward. The*
> *way our brain works is that dopamine - the so-called feel-good*
> *chemical - is released the second we actually do something. So*
> *the motivation doesn't come before, it comes after." [4]*

Indeed, it's dopamine that urges us to complete a project when a large chunk of it has already been done. It's the dopamine that nudges you to continue running a marathon when you already completed most of it, despite the fact that you are exhausted and all of your limbs ache.

One important area where dopamine is heavily involved is the domain of social interactions. Humans are social animals, because being social was absolutely critical to the survival of the species. Therefore a successful social interaction will induce dopamine response. [5]

Those are the good qualities of dopamine and this is how nature intended it to work. But those qualities that make dopamine the main element of addiction.

Have you ever been in a situation where you consumed way more alcohol than you intended at a party? Perhaps you remember the feeling. You have a drink and you feel good. But something in the back of your mind keeps telling you that if you have another one, you'll feel even better. So you have another one. And then the same thing happens. And it continues until you have had one drink too many.

Well, that's precisely what it feels like when dopamine kicks in. It doesn't give you much enjoyment on its own, but it makes you think that a great enjoyment is just around the corner: it makes you feel the anticipation of a reward. And that's what keeps you engaged in an action, even if your rational mind realizes that the action is not in your best interest.

It's the same reason why gambling is so addictive. When a player keeps pulling that lever on a slot machine, it's not a rational thought of being able to win that keeps them going. It's the feeling that next time they pull the lever, the winning combination may finally come up. Once again, it's dopamine that makes them feel this.

In many types of addictions, the subconscious mind of an addict will register any pleasant activity, as it will perceive it as something important to the survival of the body. Then, whenever this activity enters into your awareness, the subconscious mind will release dopamine to make you want to engage in the activity again.

It could be absolutely anything that makes you feel good. It could be alcohol or illicit substances. It could be video games. Or it could be social media.

What do you feel when you keep scrolling down your Twitter feed? You feel like there is something interesting just one scroll away. This is why it's so hard to stop.

How hard is it to see a number on your notification bell and not click on it? Again, in the moment, it feels like there might be something interesting or important. It's next to impossible not to click on it. Even if you use your willpower and not click on it, you will probably carry on thinking about what those notifications could have been, so you will probably end up giving in and opening your notification anyway. It will be hard to focus on work when you know that somebody responded to some of your content on social media.

This link between social media usage and dopamine release has been experimentally proven many times, so there is absolutely no doubt that social media is addictive and that it's dopamine that's responsible for this addiction. For example, one study found that, in some users, social media causes the same parts of the brain to light up that normally light up during cocaine consumption. And the extent to which they light up was the same too. Those parts of the brain were known to be activated by dopamine. **[6]**

So, there is no doubt that social media can trigger as much dopamine as hard addictive drugs. In fact, Addiction Center, an organization that helps people with addictions to find help, has said that, according to neuroscience research available to it, the effect of social media on the brain can be compared to pure dopamine being injected into the body with a syringe. [7]

And it's not an accident that social media activities trigger dopamine release. It's not only software developers that work for social media companies. They employ human behavior specialists too. Therefore social media is addictive by design.

How social media is deliberately designed to be addictive

We already know that successful social interactions trigger dopamine response. And this is the mechanism that any social media network sends into overdrive.

Naturally, each of us has around 150 acquaintances on average. We can't have too many, because there is only so much time we can dedicate to face-to-face interactions. But social media has removed this limit.

It's not uncommon to have hundreds, or even thousands, of personal connections on Facebook or Instagram. And when you express your thoughts on one of these platforms, it's not just a small circle of people that will see it. It could be many thousand.

When you interact with thousands of people, it's expected that at least some of them will respond. And at least some of these interactions will be interpreted by our subconscious as successful. And this will keep triggering dopamine response, so you will keep coming back for more.

This is why, even before any targetted behavior-modifying tricks are applied by developers, any social media platform would have a potential to be addictive. But it's not 2004 anymore and people no longer get addicted to social media by accident. Many behavior-modifying tricks have indeed been applied to the popular platforms over the years.

The seemingly benign things social media does to modify your behavior

In 2020, a documentary called "The Social Dilemma" was released on Netflix. In this film, a group of people who were formerly employed by social media companies, told the public all the details of how social media was deliberately designed to be addictive. [8]

And those participants weren't just minor rank-and-file employees. They worked in top positions in social media companies and other tech giants that use similar algorithms to the ones that social media companies use. One of the participants, Tristan Haris, is a former Google Design Ethicist. Another participant, Tim Kendall, is a former Facebook executive and a former president of Pinterest. Other participants are of a similar caliber too.

Some of the people featured in the film were the original inventors of those social media features that were then found to be addictive, such as the "like" button and infinite scroll. Some features have indeed originated as good user experience solutions and were only discovered to be addictive by accident. However, the reason why many of such features were kept was precisely because they keep the user drawn in.

"Like" button is one of the most basic features of social media that has been there right from the beginning. And perhaps it's the most benign one compared to other little widgets. However, someone "liking" your post acts as a social approval; therefore it's interpreted by our brains as a reward. Therefore posting something on social media and anticipating "likes" still triggers dopamine response.

When someone likes your post, you feel a little bit of pleasure. When you get a lot of likes, you experience a lot more pleasure. This is why even such a little thing as the "like" button has the power of making you post more, so you can get more likes.

Your timeline with infinite scroll is a much more powerful tool in terms of getting the users addicted. The inventor of the infinite scroll feature, Aza Raskin, who was also featured in "The Social Dilemma" film, later regretted his invention. And that's precisely because this is one of the most addictive features of social media. [9]

When social media just became popular, this feature didn't exist at all. You would always see the latest content that your friends have posted and you would only see a limited amount of it. If you would have kept scrolling down, you would eventually reach the end.

But infinite scroll, the content will never end. You can keep scrolling and scrolling and scrolling. And the content will keep coming up.

Plus, these days, it's not only the content that has been posted by your friends that will appear on your timeline. You will see seemingly random content from the groups you are a member of. You will see various ads. And you will see content that Facebook recommends to you based on your preferences.

The combination of the facts that the content is seemingly random and it never ends is precisely what triggers a strong dopamine response. You never know what kind of content you will encounter if you'll just keep scrolling down. At some point, you ought to encounter something interesting. And you can keep doing that ad infinitum. This is why, out of all social media widgets, infinite scroll is probably the one that is responsible for the largest amount of hours wasted.

But it doesn't stop there. Any other widget that defines modern-day social media that you can think of has been designed as a tool to keep you hooked. For example, an animation that shows you when someone is typing a message was designed just for this purpose.

Back in the days, when you posted something, you had no way of knowing that someone had responded until someone did. But these days, you will instantly see an animation as soon as someone has started typing. This animation incentivizes you to stay on the platform until the response from the other person is complete. You know that this is about to happen soon, so you would not want to just leave the platform and check on it later.

Same goes for the notification bell. When you see a number on it (especially if this number is brightly colored and stands out from its background), dopamine response in your brain will be initiated. You will want to click on it to see what's there. This is precisely why this number was designed to be instantly noticeable.

Social media views its users as lab pigeons

Most of the standard social media components rely on the concept of variable reward. This is when you are compelled by your subconscious to take a particular action, because this action may or may not result in the reward. You don't know what the reward will be and you don't even know if there will be a reward at all. But the possibility that there might be some kind of a reward is precisely what excites our brain. And the fact that the reward is variable rather than consistent is known to result in compulsive behavior.

This concept is not new. It came from experiments with pigeons that Dr Skinner, a famous American psychologist, conducted in the 1950s. He placed pigeons in a compartment , which later became known as the "Skinner Box". Inside this compartment, there was a button and an opening. [10]

In the first part of the experiment, food would appear every time the pigeon would peck the button. This would make the pigeon peck the button at fairly regular intervals.

But then, Dr Skinner made a tweak. Insead of delivering food every time the button is pecked, it would be delivered after a random number of pecks. And then, something interesting happened.

Pigeons started pecking the button compulsively. Some even started to peck it non-stop for up to 16 hours straight! And the less frequent the reward was - the more frequent was the pecking.

This experiment was then replicated with rats and other animals with similar results. And now, with social media, the same experiment is conducted at a large scale on humans.

Humans have much better impulse control compared to any other animals. But still, we have the same dopamine-based reward system as any other animal has. Therefore any process that involves variable rewards would still be effective to develop compulsive behavior in humans.

A gambling addict is no different from a pigeon from Dr Skinner's experiment. He will keep compulsively pulling the lever on a slot machine until he runs out of money, despite not winning much. But so is someone who carries on compulsively scrolling Facebook timeline.

You may only have a small amount of interactions on social media that are genuinely positive. Perhaps, only a small proportion of the content you see there is in any way interesting. But just like that pigeon, you will keep scrolling and refreshing your notifications in case you come across something interesting.

But above all of these, social media companies employ the best user experience experts. This is why all of these platforms are designed to be extremely easy to use. Good UX is generally a good thing, but not when it's applied to a system that is designed to be addictive and trigger compulsive behavior.

And those experts that social media companies employ do indeed perform experiments on their users, just like Dr Skinner did on his pigeons. In 2014 Facebook got caught conducting an experiment with 689,000 of its users. The algorithms were tweaked to limit exposure to either positive or negative content, depending on which group the unwilling participants were in. The study was conducted to see how users' emotions could be manipulated. [11]

This is just one experiment out of many. And we only know about it, because the information was leaked out. But it's safe to assume there are many more experiments like this that have been done in secret.

So, here is clear evidence that the algorithms on social media are explicitly designed to show you the content that will make you behave the way social media wants you to, which means spending as much time on their platform as possible. It doesn't necessarily imply that that's the content that will make you happy. All that's important is that you keep seeing the content that keeps you engaged, even if it makes you sad or angry.

An activity that is easy to do will not trigger inner resistance from your subconscious mind. And if, on top of that, the abovementioned activity is also perceived by your brain as rewarding, then you will also feel an incredibly strong pull towards this activity. And that makes all addictive mechanisms behind it even more powerful.

But as a software developer, you are especially susceptible to all these manipulative mechanisms. Here is why.

Why programmers are especially susceptible to social media addiction

As a programmer, your main tools of trade are a computer and the internet connection. But these tools are also the exact medium through which social media is delivered to its users.

Brain activity consumes a lot of energy. And because we have evolved in an environment where our next meal wasn't guaranteed, our instincts have evolved to conserve as much energy as possible.

This precise feature of our physiology is the reason why social media is especially dangerous to software developers. The work that we do is hard. But the same machine that we write our code on, which earns us money and progresses our careers, also has access to social media websites, the biggest source of temptations that can easily derail your career progress. And social media was deliberately designed to be extremely easy to use. So, when our brain needs to choose between writing code or visiting social media, the latter proposition will be much more attractive to it.

This problem becomes especially big if you already have a habit of using social media on the computer you do your work on. At the first glance, having a short break now and then to watch some memes that your friends have sent you may seem like an innocent passtime. But over time, it can become a truly destructive habit.

No alcoholic has ever intended to become an alcoholic. They started with just a few drinks now and again. But over time, a habit of excessive drinking was formed. It's same with social media. It was deliberately designed to be as addictive as alcohol. So, just like it is with alcohol, occasional use of it can evolve into a constant compulsive usage that takes over your life. It's especially true when it was incredibly easy to access.

If you have been regularly accessing your social media feed from the same computer you do your work on, your brain would be accustomed to it. And to the brain, it's the activity that it will want to engage in due to its strong effect on your brain's reward system.

Programming, on the other hand, is an activity that you have to deliberately teach your brain to love. It's hard, so your brain will not want to do it automatically. You might be a tech enthusiast, but to really fall in love with programming, you need to achieve several wins in this field. You will have to become good at coding and successfully develop a number of pieces of fully functioning software. A completed task that required a lot of work is rewarding to our brain. But you need to complete a number of tasks of a particular type to teach your brain to associate the task with a reward.

So, on one hand, you have an activity that will only start to feel truly rewarding to your brain after a lot of effort. On the other hand, you have an activity that will be perceived as rewarding right away with no any effort at all. Which activity do you think your brain will prefer?

Because one of the primary goals of our brain is to conserve energy, the subconscious mind will always choose the path of least resistance. So, unless you consciously apply some willpower, an activity that was deliberately designed to be as friction-free as possible will always win over a task that is hard to do. But you only have so much willpower. You can't keep applying it forever

And at what point your willpower is depleted the most? It's when your overall mental energy is depleted. And nothing depletes the mental energy as much as the heavy cognitive work that you'll have to perform as a programmer.

So, as a programmer, you are especially vulnerable to be consumed by the addictive mechanisms of social media. Even if you are a person with a good capacity to control your impulses, this capacity all but disappears when your brain is tired.

When your brain is tired, things like visiting social media become incredibly tempting. It's right there, right at your fingertips. And when something that your brain perceives as rewarding is easily within your reach and you no longer have a capacity to resist it, you will probably end up visiting it on autopilot.

Every time you visit it, you will contribute a little into building neural pathways for this action. And over time, those pathways will become strong. As the habit becomes stronger, you will require more willpower to resist it. Therefore habitual usage of social media when you are trying to do productive work may make any kind of productive work a lot harder.

This is why nothing has a bigger capacity to derail your programming career than social media.

Granted, not everyone gets completely addicted to social media, just like not every drinker becomes an alcoholic. There are plenty of people who can use Facebook several times throughout the day for years and still become highly productive and highly successful at what they do.

But even if you don't develop a fully-fledged addiction to it, chances are that you will still habitually use it more than you intended to. Anything that's designed to be addictive will at least form a strong habit.

Even if you are the lucky one and you manage not to develop a strong social media habit despite its regular use, it's still a source of distraction. You would still probably be more successful if you never alternated its use with your work.

This is why it's better not to ever log into any of your social media accounts on the same device you work on unless you absolutely have to. There are still valid uses for social media (which we will discuss later in **chapter 5**), but it's better to use it on devices that are separate from the ones you do your work on. As we discussed before, this will enable you to create a distraction-free environment that is conducive to deep work.

Likewise, it also pays to not use social media at all during your working hours. If you keep it up for long enough, to your brain, this will become a habit. If, for example, you have only been checking your Twitter after 6PM, your subconscious will stop even suggesting that you should do it earlier. Or maybe that nudge will still remain there forever, but it will be so weak that you'll be able to easily deal with it.

Perhaps, the worst thing about social media is that it's something that can quickly offset all the productive habits that you have spent so much time and effort building. And that's what you need to pay especially close attention to.

How social media can easily offset productive habits

The process of habit-formation is similar to cultivating a garden.

Productive habits are like garden plants. They require time and conscious effort to be cultivated. You cannot build a productive habit unless you keep deliberately practicing the actions required for its formation.

Destructive habits, on the other hand, are like weeds in your garden. They will sprout up on their own without any effort on your part at all. You will need to constantly be on the lookout for any new ones, so you can eradicate them while they are still small.

Well, in the context of this metaphor, social media habit is like one of those weeds that are next to impossible to get rid of once they take hold. Social media is as powerful as Japanese Knotweed or Himalayan Balsam. These weeds can take over your garden quickly and can even damage your structures. Eradicating them is very hard and very expensive.

Remember that social media was deliberately designed to form strong neural pathways very quickly. And those get formed with no effort from yourself. At one point, you are simply using social media to show your photos to your friends, chat with them and watch some funny memes. It can't get any more benign than that. But it really isn't. Gradually, if you are not careful, you may end up opening your social media app compulsively.

If a strong neural pathway was formed with hardly any effort, demolishing this neural pathway will be a long and hard process. It's a lot easier for impulses to travel along a well-established path than it is via the path that you are only trying to build. And those impulses will keep reinforcing the path, which in turn, will keep reinforcing the behavior that this pathway is responsible for.

So, you don't just have to work hard to build a strong productive habit that your brain doesn't particularly want you to build. You will have to do it while trying to demolish another strong habit that is already well-established. Once a destructive habit takes hold and becomes strong, the effort required to build a productive habit to counteract it will be several degrees of magnitude greater than it would have been otherwise.

This is why, if you want to become an elite-level software developer, it's absolutely imperative that you are fully aware of all the dangers of social media. You need to be aware that all the shiny UI components that you interact with aren't there just to improve your experience. They are there primarily to get you hooked.

Just like Hymalayan Balsam weed is easy enough to eradicate if you spot it early enough, social media usage can be prevented from becoming a compulsive habit once you spot early signs of a potential problem.

All these habit-forming widgets that you interact with are designed to bypass your rational analysis. They were made to interact with you on an instinctual level. This is why problem usage of social media often only becomes apparent when it's already a fairly well-established habit.

But if you want to become a truly elite software developer, it may take far less than what's generally considered to be problem usage to interfere with your efforts. Even relatively mild social media usage can do it.

For example, you might be a reasonably good programmer. You might have been using social media for years and, so far, it hasn't prevented you from reaching certain goals in your career. Perhaps, your social media usage is limited to checking Facebook every so often throughout the day and you have no problem putting your smartphone down whenever you need to.

But what if the action of looking at your social media prevents you from ever entering the state of flow and doing any deep work? Of course, you still can write code, even if you aren't in the state of flow. But just imagine how much more productive would be a developer who regularly enters the state of flow compared to you? How much quicker can someone complete a task if they don't have a habit of interrupting themselves?

Yes, social media would not prevent you from having a decent job. But it can easily prevent you from getting to the elite level.

When you want to perform at an elite level, you absolutely have to fine-tune your routine. Any mildly bad habit that is generally acceptable in the society can be sufficient to prevent you from becoming an elite.

Elite sportspeople, for example, don't only spend countless hours training. They also religiously watch what they eat and make sure they sleep enough. Quite a few of them go to extreme length to make sure they win competitions. **[12]**

If you want to achieve something of value, you always have to sacrifice something. And if you want to become a world-class programmer, the most important thing that you need to work on are your habits. So, anything that prevents you from building the right habits needs to get sacrificed.

Yes, it's true that many people in society are highly functioning social media addicts. And that doesn't seem to be preventing them from having a reasonable quality of life. They aren't like drug addicts that you can see on street corners begging for change.

But remember that the vast majority of people are content with merely average lives. And regular social media usage might be just fine to live an average life. But elite programmers are not merely average. So, what's acceptable for an average person would not necessarily be acceptable for them.

So, what you need to do is to make sure that social media usage doesn't become a subconscious habit. It would be a good idea to monitor how much social media you use to spot any early signs of it becoming a hindrance to your goals.

What you can do, for example, is monitor how much time you spend on it and whether or not it's increasing over time. Of course, you can't just trust yourself to put a timewatch on every time you log into your Instagram. But what you can do is install a dedicated app on your smartphone or a browser plugin on your computer to do it for you. And then you can check the patterns over time.

There are plenty of apps and browser plugins that do this. Social Fever, Offtime and Web Time Tracker are some of the examples. They are all pretty similar to each other and are simple to use. But despite their simplicity, they are extremely useful. Those are the best tools to prevent proverbial Knotweed from taking over your garden while it still can be stopped.

How to use social media without allowing it to use you

So, if social media is so addictive, would I suggest that you need to stop using it completely? Well, not necessarily.

Of course, if you suffer from a genuine social media addiction and you have very little impulse control while interacting with it, then perhaps going cold turkey would be a good idea. Maybe it would even be useful to completely delete all of your profiles. But for an average social media user, such drastic actions won't be necessary.

Not everything about social media is bad. Yes, it has been designed to get you hooked. But it also provided us with many useful tools that didn't exist before. It's social media that makes it easy to share your thoughts with countless people everywhere around the globe. Because of social media, it's easier to build your personal brand than it ever was. And there are many other useful things that you can engage in courtesy of social media that will help you to build your career or to just enhance the overall quality of your life.

So, quitting social media completely might not be the best course of action. But the trick is to use social media without letting it to use you.

But how would you go about doing this? Well, I would start with the recommendations that were made by participants of "The Social Dilemma" film. But as the film covered many problems from bg tech industry, I will focus on only those recommendations that counteract the habit-forming mechanisms that social media employs.

1. **Delete unnecessary apps**. Less apps there are - less distraction there is. You probably won't be a regular user of all social media networks. So why keep those apps that you rarely use? It's much easier than just switching off notifications in each one of them individually so they don't unnecessarily distract you. Plus, if you still need to use any of those networks now and then, you can still log into them via your browser.

2. **Turn off your notifications**. On my smartphone, I have completely disabled all notifications on all social media apps. I still have them on messengers, so my phone still rings when someone tries to contact me. But I won't get notified if anyone has commented on one of my posts. I need to proactively open my timeline to see those.

3. **Fine-tune in-app notifications while you are using a social media network.** While you should switch off external notifications in social media apps completely, there is still a value in using those in-app notifications that you will only see when you actually open the app. But those still need to be fine-tuned. For example, I would switch off all notifications, except the ones that tell me if someone has commented on my post, replied to my comment or tagged me. Maybe it would make sense to keep birthday notifications too. But I don't get notified when someone I don't know posts something in a group that I'm a member of.

4. **Don't follow recommended content.** If a social media network uses a recommendation engine, like YouTube does, then a good idea would be not to click on any recommended content. Clicking on recommendations facilitates the

formation of a strong habit, similar to the one that is facilitated by continuously scrolling down through your timeline. And it can take you down a rabbit hole where you can binge-watch many videos that just happened to have been recommended to you.

5. **Have a plan for what you need to do and for how long.** On websites like YouTube, it's better to have a plan. When you visit the site, have an idea in your head on what kind of video you would like to watch. And then just search for that specific type of videos. And, once done, just leave the site. For this, it would also make sense to turn the autoplay feature off, so another randomly selected video that is similar to the one that you just watched doesn't get played automatically.

6. **Use browser tools to reduce recommended content**. Because it's not only YouTube that has recommendations, perhaps it would make sense to eradicate them on all sites that you visit. And to do so, you can download a browser extension, such as AdBlock Plus.

7. **Recognize and avoid obvious clickbait.** Clickbait is any content that has a title that has been designed to trigger a strong emotional response. After seeing this title, most people would automatically click on the link and read the story.

   Examples of clickbait titles could be the following:

   "How to Achieve Results Using This One Weird Trick"

   "This is what the government has been hiding from you"

   "A trick that car insurers don't want you to know"

   Clickbait title doesn't necessarily mean that the content is of poor quality and isn't helpful. Every publisher is using clickbait these days, because it's the only way to be heard among a huge volume of noise. But be aware that such a thing exists and try not to click on any titles that sound obviously exaggerated. In fact, try to avoid following profiles that post a lot of content with such titles.

8. **Limit screen time.** Another great recommendation is to limit the screen time that you dedicate to social media. You already know that there are plenty of mobile apps and browser plugins that measure your screen time. Some of them can be configured to notify you if you have spent a particular amount of time on specific types of activity. So, if you want to limit the amount of time you spend on social media, you can use these tools.

9. **Protect some time each day**. It makes sense not to use social media at all during specific times of day. I wouldn't use it the first thing in the morning. It's also prudent not to use it during working hours. Your brain will then get accustomed to this and you won't even have cravings to check your timeline while you are working on that difficult problem. It will become your routine and social media will not interfere with your work activities at all.

Then, there are some techniques that I have personally discovered that worked very well for me. Perhaps you could consider those.

1. **Unfollow anyone who regularly posts content that triggers a strong disagreement in you.**

   You don't necessarily have to block them or remove them from your connection list. Perhaps you know them in real life and still want to be friends. Perhaps they are good people to talk to in person. But on social media, they post a lot of content that upsets you one way or another.

   And that's precisely what the "unfollow" button is for. You will still be connected, but the stuff that they post will stop appearing on your timeline.

   At the first glance, this advice sounds contrary to what participants of "The Social Dilemma" have recommended. They have said that following those you disagree with is a good thing. That's how you end up not being dragged into an echo chamber. And that's what prevents your worldview from getting completely biased.

But this is not necessarily a contradiction. Seeing opinions you disagree with is one thing. But it's an entirely different thing if those opinions are expressed in an aggressive manner. Or perhaps those opinions are something you deeply disagree with on a fundamental level.

If you see such content, it may trigger a strong emotional reaction in you. And then, you might not be able to fully focus on your other activities. You will carry on thinking about it for a while.

We aren't talking about broadening your perspective right now. We are talking about becoming an elite programmer. And the content that has a power of affecting your focus is a huge problem in this context.

Therefore, by all means, follow those you disagree with. But try to select only those who present their opinion in a respectful manner and are capable of backing their opinion up with facts. Unfollow the rest.

2. **Deliberately seek useful content that will aid you with achieving your goals.** Over time, the algorithms will figure out that this is the content that you prefer, so you will get more of such content delivered. And that's, perhaps, the only exception to the rule of not clicking on the content that was delivered to you by a recommendation engine.

3. **Have at least one day per week of a complete social media detox.** This is one of the best things you can do for yourself. On that day when you aren't allowed to use any social media at all, you will notice straight away how much more productive you are.

By following the above advice, you will build an immunity to all the addictive mechanisms of social media. You will build a habit to use social media only when you consciously choose to do so. After some time, getting you into autopilot mode to mindlessly browse your feed will become impossible.

Now you know what is the biggest enemy in your environment that you must avoid in order to become a successful programmer. Now, we will move on to some meta-skills that you can develop to help you. And the meta-skill that can help you stand out is getting into a state of deep focus. Make this a habit and you're on your way to being an exceptional programmer.

References

1. Cal Newport - Digital Minimalism: Choosing a Focused Life in a Noisy World - Portfolio
2. Nir Eyal - Hooked: How to Build Habit-Forming Products - Portfolio Penguin
3. John Medina - Brain Rules, Updated and Expanded: 12 Principles for Surviving and Thriving at Work, Home, and School - Pear Press
4. Brendon Burchard - The Motivation Manifesto: 9 Declarations to Claim Your Personal Power - Hay House Inc
5. Deborah Oakley - Only the lonely – a surprise role for dopamine in social interplay - London Institute of Medical Science
6. Jena Hilliard - New Study Suggests Excessive Social Media Use Is Comparable To Drug Addiction - Addiction Center
7. Jena Hilliard - What Is Social Media Addiction? - Addiction Center
8. The Social Dilemma - Netflix Documentary, 2020
9. Hilary Andersson - Social media apps are 'deliberately' addictive to users - BBC Panorama
10. Björn Lindström - Social media as a modern-day Skinner Box? - Journal of Behavioral and Social Sciences
11. Kashmir Hill - Facebook Manipulated 689,003 Users' Emotions For Science - Forbes, Jun 28, 2014
12. Bradley Popkin - How Fighters Aggressively Lose Weight Before Weigh-in - Men's Journal

CHAPTER 2

YOUR ALLIES – DEEP WORK AND THE STATE OF FLOW

Only through focus can you do world-class things, no matter how capable you are.
—Bill Gates, a co-founder of Microsoft

Good programming habits are essential for being a great programmer. And there are many different habits that you need to master to put yourself way above most of your competition: writing your code according to best practices; creating productive routines; and surrounding yourself with cues that will help to keep procrastination at bay. These habits help you to improve your performance by automating your actions, which, to some extent, automates your output. And these habits alone will make you stand out from the crowd. But a specific skill that will make you stand out even more is knowing how to get into the state of deep work.

When you acquire the habit of setting aside all distractions while you work, you have made it easier and quicker to complete the task that you were planning to complete. Add this to the fact you have already developed the skill to produce well-written code on autopilot. But when you merely work on autopilot, you will still be thinking about the things that have nothing to do with your work. Remember how sometimes you can't remember making a journey in your car because you were driving on autopilot and thinking about other things?

Autopilot is fine, but it would be much better (and much more enjoyable) if you could focus entirely on the task that you are doing.

The quality of the output will then go over the roof and there will be a smaller chance of bugs creeping into your code. This will also help you to complete the task quicker, which will make it easier to stick to the schedule and increase the overall performance metrics. Likewise, your work-life balance will improve if you can achieve more within a shorter period of time. The process of dedicating your entire focus to the task at hand is known as "deep work". And there is a mental state that is conducive to it.

Achieving a certain mental state may sound well outside of your comfort zone. But what if I told you that the ability to enter that mental state is in itself nothing but a habit? What if I told you that you can learn to enter it almost at will? And what if I told you that mastering the skill of doing highly focused work will improve the overall quality of your life?

Why deep work matters to your success as a programmer

The ability to do deep work is an acquired skill. It has to be consciously developed through finding the optimum mental state and building the right habits to help you get there. Mastering it takes time, just like it takes time to build any other productive habit. But, once mastered, it will make building the other right habits easier.

It's very common for programmers to listen to something in the background while working. Many struggle to focus on a single activity for too long and they regularly take breaks to browse the web or do any other unproductive activities. This is the opposite of the concept of "deep work" - when all undivided attention is fully focused on a single task for a prolonged period of time.

Coincidentally, the term "deep work" has actually originated from computer science. It was coined by Calvin C. Newport, who is an associate professor of computer science at Georgetown University and a bestselling non-fiction author. In fact, "Deep Work" happens to be the name of one of his best-known books.

Why he thinks the ability to do deep work is important can be summarized by this quote from his book, which says there are, *"Two*

Core Abilities for Thriving in the New Economy 1. The ability to quickly master hard things. 2. The ability to produce at an elite level, in terms of both quality and speed.". [1]

To master hard things, you have all the time in the world. But to master them quickly, you need to focus for long periods at a time. For this, you need the ability to do deep work.

The speed at which you master hard things is especially relevant for any career in the IT sector, including programming. It's not a secret that technology evolves at a rapid pace. Therefore, if you are too slow to learn something, the stuff that you have spent so much effort learning becomes irrelevant once you master it.

Likewise, to be able to produce at the elite level, where the output is both quick and of high quality, you need to be able to focus. Yes, you can produce things quickly without much focus. But you will probably overlook something in the process, which will introduce defects into your output or otherwise reduce the overall quality of it.

Finally, another advantage of being able to pay undivided attention to your work is that this ability is relatively rare. Not many developers consciously study it. Therefore, if you master it, you will stand out. Your performance will be visibly better than that of your competitors. And you will probably be making less mistakes and introducing less bugs than them.

Why deep work isn't something we are naturally good at

But there is a reason achieving the optimum mental state that allows you to do deep work isn't commonplace: our brains are not naturally built to do it. Our natural instinct would be to provide as little focus as possible to something that is intellectually challenging to conserve that all important energy. And brains don't like boredom either. So, unless you consciously cultivate the habit of deep work, you will probably be among the ranks of those who regularly procrastinate and never pay 100% attention to any work-related task. [2]

Remember how Anatoly Karpov lost 10 kg (or 22 pounds) of bodyweight during the chess tournament of 1984 purely because of intense focus on the game? That's precisely why our bodies don't like to keep our brains focused and will do anything to try to preserve the energy. But the irony is that by forcing yourself to try maintaining the focus while your body is telling you not to is probably something that will waste even more energy.

Because programming is intellectually challenging, the best and quickest way to solve a programming problem is by fully focusing on it. To solve pretty much any programming problem other than copy-pasting boilerplate code, you will have to create some abstract steps in your head that would lead to the solution. And this is hard to do if your attention is split between this problem and somewhere else.

If you struggle to maintain your undivided focus on a problem, you may still be able to solve it, but it will probably take you longer than it would be for someone who gave it 100% of focus. And if you constantly jump between work and something else, you will have to rebuild all the abstract models in your head every time you return to the problem. It wastes a lot of effort and mental energy. People who haven't made deep work their habit often feel mentally-drained towards the end of the working day.

Repeatedly shifting attention between work, news and social media is known as context switching or multitasking. [3] Those who are acquainted with how computer processors work, will be familiar with what context switching is. In a nutshell, it's about running multiple threads and switching between them, while each thread maintains its state. It's something that should be avoided, as it slows down a computer's performance. [4] Even though every single context switch doesn't take a lot of mental energy, doing many of them throughout the day makes the wasted energy add up. The tiredness towards the end of your day will be almost guaranteed.

Context switching also significantly slows down the performance of the brain in a similar way that it slows down computer performance. This is why pretty much all psychologists, management consultants and productivity coaches unanimously agree that it's bad. The reason why it is bad is the same as with computers. When a thread gets suspended to execute another thread, the resources need to be dedicated to save the state of the original thread. Likewise, when you switch from one task to another, the residue of your original task remains in the brain.

Of course, there is nothing wrong with listening to something in the background while you are doing some basic set-up task or copying some boilerplate code. These sorts of tasks aren't challenging, so your performance won't be affected by some nice music or a podcast. In fact, it might actually be useful to play something in the background in this case to make sure that you don't get excessively bored and lose your focus completely. But those types of tasks are special cases and perhaps the only exception.

Doing deep work is challenging at first – as we've seen above the brain isn't naturally wired to desire deep work. And it takes more than developing routines or forming habits. The best way to do it is to learn to get into a special mental state that will make it easy.

Why the ability to do deep work depends on your mental state

An important point about deep work is that it's best done when you aren't in the same mood as you are while you aren't working. You aren't focused on a single thing most of the time throughout the day. When we are in a normal semi-relaxed state, our attention wanders between different parts of our external environment and our internal thoughts. So, in order to start deep work, you will need to shift into a different mental state.

This is why the hardest thing about deep work is to start it. Suddenly, all the stimuli that you were normally surrounded by temporarily cease to exist. And while your mind was wandering freely just a minute ago, you are now trying to focus it. You will feel bored. And this is precisely why that's the time when you will probably get the strongest possible urge to procrastinate.

If deep work was easy, it would not be called "the superpower of the 21st century" by Calvin C. Newport, the author of "Deep Work". This is what else he says about it: *"Deep work is hard and shallow work is easier and in the absence of clear goals for your job, the visible busyness that surrounds shallow work becomes self-preserving." [1]*

But how exactly do you get into the mental state that's conducive to working deep? Well, certainly not by willing it to happen. Alteration of your mental state is not what you will have to consciously think of. It will happen on its own. But you will need to start on your task and stay fully occupied by it for at least 15-20 minutes for this to happen. And that's the hardest part. But on occasions, acquiring and maintaining focus happens almost involuntarily.

Everyone is familiar with a situation where they didn't feel like doing something. But after actually starting on the task, they haven't even noticed how they eventually became fully occupied by it. But right at the beginning, they were probably still thinking about the things they were doing before they got started. That's an example of the mental residue left in your brain from context switching. And this is why you will probably have a short period of time (10-15 minutes) when you will have to consciously force yourself to focus. Then, once your brain has adjusted, you will just get on with it.

But if you have allowed yourself to build a bad habit of procrastinating every time you feel like it, you may never enter the required mental state. And, as a consequence, you won't really learn how to do any deep work. This is a very dangerous habit that may cost you your career. And, just like any other nasty habit, it will appear like a weed without any effort from your side, as long as you aren't consciously addressing it.

But if you have successfully managed to get into the state of deep work on a regular basis, it will start becoming easier and easier. Partially, because repeated action will build the relevant neural pathways in your brain. But also because you will get familiar with the productive mental state of deep work and you will start enjoying it and seeing it as an opportunity for growth.

Scott Hanselman, a famous senior software engineer from Microsoft who is known for his hyper-productivity, has deliberately designed his working routine to make getting into the state of flow easily. He practices aggressive elimination of all distractions and this is what he repeatedly attributed to his success. These are some of his quotes about the importance of it:

> *"Remember that anything important that happens in the world, in the news, in your life, in your work , will come your (way) many times, if there's another 9-11, somebody will tell you. You probably didn't learn it by hitting refresh on your favorite news site."*

> *"Be wrapped up like a child in the thing that captures your attention, get that excitement back, and that excitement does not involve Alt-Tabbing over to Gmail."*

Perhaps, it will even become some sort of an addiction. And you will start looking forward to your next "fix". But if an addiction can make you work better, improve your pay, career prospects and work–life balance, it's certainly not a bad addiction to have.

There is even a scientific name for the mental state that is conducive to deep work - the state of flow. Likewise, there are scientifically-proven reasons why doing deep work in this state is something that you will enjoy.

The state of flow – a trance-like mental state of high productivity

You may have already heard the expression of "being in the zone" or "experiencing the state of flow". For example, a basketball player may execute a perfect throw. Or a musician may perform a perfect cover of some song. Perfect execution of some action is just an outward expression of the state of flow. What's more important is what happens on the inside - inside your head. The state of flow is an altered state of consciousness. The actions are just the symptoms of that.

When you are "in the zone", it feels like time doesn't exist. You do things spontaneously, but it's very different from doing things subconsciously on an autopilot. In the state of flow, you are fully aware of your actions. And it just happens that you perform the right actions at the right time. This is why it's called "the state of flow".

Instead of constantly thinking what to do next, you just do what your body wants you to do. It's just going with the flow instead of fighting the current.

And it's not just some sort of metaphysical mumbo-jumbo that happens only to some highly-impressionable people. The state of flow is real. It was discovered by science and the whole branch of science was developed to study it.

First named by prominent psychologist Mihaly Csikszentmihalyi in 1975, it was discovered by studying high-level performers, such as artists. The best-performing ones seemed to be able to get lost in their work. And they enjoyed the experience.

And it's not an accident that Csikszentmihalyi dedicated his life to studying this emotional state. He grew up in Europe during World War 2 and, as a kid, he saw the amount of misery that the war has caused. And, as he said in one of his best-known TED talks, this is how he got interested in this type of research:

> *"I grew up in Europe, and World War II caught me when I was between seven and 10 years old. And I realized how few of the grown-ups that I knew were able to withstand the tragedies that the war visited on them -- how few of them could even resemble a normal, contented, satisfied, happy life once their job, their home, their security was destroyed by the war. So I became interested in understanding what contributed to a life that was worth living. And I tried, as a child, as a teenager, to read philosophy and to get involved in art and religion and many other ways that I could see as a possible answer to that question. And finally I ended up encountering psychology by chance." [5]*

Eventually, after interviewing and examining countless people, Mihaly Csikszentmihalyi and his team determined that it wasn't merely an accident of birth or some lucky circumstances that made people go into this mental state. The state was replicable and pretty much any reasonably healthy individual was capable of entering it. Moreover, the state had a number of measurable and consistent characteristics.

These six components that are always present during the flow experience were identified:

- Concentration that is intensely focused on the present moment

- Action and awareness are perceived to be one

- Sense of self disappears

- A strong sense of control over the present situation

- Distorted perception of time

- Sense of pleasure from the activity being performed

State of flow requires all of these components. If any of these is absent, you aren't really in the state of flow. **[6]**

The reason why state of flow limits parts of your perception (losing sense of self, sense of time being distorted, etc.) is because the human brain has a limited capacity to process the information. We simply can't pay attention to everything that's happening in our environment at any point of time. It's way too much. So we only focus on those bits of information that are relevant.

But when you are in the state of flow, your entire focus is allocated to a single activity that you are engaged in. Nothing outside of it exists to your perception. And this is why, although you perform most optimally while you are experiencing the flow, you may become completely oblivious to any other potentially important things. But this is also what prevents you from being distracted. As Csikszentmihalyi said:

> *"Well, when you are really involved in this completely engaging process of creating something new, as this man is, he doesn't have enough attention left over to monitor how his body feels, or his problems at home. He can't even feel that he's hungry or tired. His body disappears, his identity disappears from his consciousness, because he doesn't have enough attention, like none of us do, to really do well something that requires a lot of concentration, and at the same time to feel that he exists. So*

existence is temporarily suspended. And he says that his hand seems to be moving by itself. "

Simply put, the mental energy that is normally dedicated to other parts of your perception are rerouted onto the activity that you are currently engaged in. Your brain is probably consuming as much energy as normal, but your task gets more of it, while everything else gets none. This is why the focus on your activity is intense, while everything else, even the perception of self, ceases to exist.

Most people have experienced the state of flow. If you are a keen gamer, you can probably remember some moments when time stood still and you were fully immersed in the game. Or maybe you took part in some extreme sports. While you were engaged in the activity, nothing seemed to exist. And you probably didn't even have to put effort into getting into this state. It just came naturally.

The top NBA players are well known for getting into the state of low on a regular basis, or "getting in the zone", as they tend to refer to it. One of the most famous players, Kobe Bryant, said the following about the process

"It's hard to describe. You just feel so confident. You get your feet set and get a good look at the basket—it's going in. Even the ones I missed I thought were going in." [7]

The good news is that it's not only the fun activities where you can experience the state of flow. You can learn to experience it while performing any creative endeavor. Writing software code just happens to be one of such activities.

But being hyper-focused on your task is not the only benefit of the flow state. Any activity that you do in this mental state feels pleasant. You just don't want to stop during this activity. And if you manage to get into this state often enough, you will start looking forward to these activities. This is precisely why truly exceptional coders love to code. It's not the syntax of any given programming language that's exciting. And it's not the logic of the program either. What they actually love is the mental state that they are in while being fully engaged in the process of coding

Learning something complex and then being able to fully immerse yourself in it gives you a sense of empowerment. This is, for example, what Scott Hanselman said about why he enjoys coding:

> *"Learning to code, to me, is no different from me having someone teach me basic woodworking, gardening, or kitchen tile. After each of these projects my sense of personal empowerment increased. In each situation I learned how to think about a problem and solve it. I can do this. I can change my world." [8]*

Another important factor is that this mental state doesn't drain much mental energy. You don't have to consciously strive to maintain hyper-focus once you've achieved this productive mental state; at this point it is self-maintaining for a long time.

All of these factors are the reason why the state of flow is the best mental state to do deep work in. But there's more to it.

Why state of flow is the easiest way to do deep work in

Deep work isn't exactly the same thing as the state of flow. Yes, these two things overlap. But deep work refers to the type of activity that you do and not the mental state you do it in.

Broadly speaking, you can be in one of three mental states while doing deep work:

- Actively trying to suppress distracting thoughts and forcing yourself to concentrate.

- Experiencing low-level boredom.

- Experiencing the flow.

Why forced focus is counterproductive

You already know that it is incredibly hard to be productive while you are trying to suppress all distracting self-talk and stimuli that prevent you from focusing on an important task. I would imagine that every software developer has been in this situation. You can probably relate to this and recognize it as a time when you are the most susceptible to procrastination.

You will be draining a lot of mental energy in the process. Therefore, unless you can manage to get into a different mental state, you won't be able to keep yourself doing deep work for long. Probably half an hour is your absolute limit. And then, you can keep trying, but there won't be much productive work done unless you take a break.

Yes, you can hush the unwanted thoughts temporarily and exhibit some focus. But then those thoughts will just come back. And they'll keep coming back until you will eventually get tired.

Tolerable low-level boredom can motivate

Low level boredom is a fairly natural mental state that many people have forgotten the feeling of due to constant hyper-stimulation by social media, video games and various other smart gadgets. This state doesn't feel entirely unpleasant and you can maintain it for a fairly long time. Most of your focus is given to the task at hand, but some of your thoughts still wander. And even though this state is highly tolerable, it still doesn't feel like it's the most pleasant thing you could be doing.

The term "low level boredom" is not used universally, but perfectly describes the mental state and distinguishes a mildly unpleasant boredom from an unbearable one. It's "high level" unbearable boredom that causes your thoughts to wander and makes concentration on important work nearly impossible.

Wijnand van Tilburg from the University of Limerick has done a lot of research on boredom and found a link between it and the desire to do meaningful, but not always pleasant, tasks. He said the following about the benefits of boredom:

> *"Boredom makes people long for different and purposeful activities, and as a result they turn towards more challenging and meaningful activities, turning towards what they perceive to be really meaningful in life, donating to charity or signing up for blood donations could not have increased the level of stimulation, interest, arousal, novelty, fun, or challenge*

50

experienced during the boring activity, simply because the boring activity finished before prosocial behavior was assessed, therefore, we show that boredom affects attitudes and behaviour even after the boring activity, if people have not had the chance to re-establish meaningfulness." [9]

This characteristic of boredom is precisely why it's a reasonably good mental state to be in while programming. Unless you are working for some genuinely unethical company, writing code would be meaningful work. but still, the state of low-level boredom is still not the perfect mental state to do coding in.

Because your attention is still somewhat split, some degree of competition between conflicting thoughts still occurs inside your head. And this competition still wastes mental energy. So you will still not be able to maintain this mental state for long. However, this time, you can probably last a couple of hours, because there isn't a lot of context switching happening in your head.

Experiencing the flow

The state of flow is the most optimal mental state of them all. Your entire attention is focused on the task at hand. Any other aspects of your environment cease to exist to your perception. And there is virtually no context switching happening.

Because the entirety of your focus is on your work, this is by far the most productive state to be in. You don't see any distractions - internal or external. All you see is the task that you are engaged in. All your mental energy is dedicated toward completion of this task.

This is why, to be as efficient as possible, you need to aim to enter the state of flow.

But don't worry if the process of getting into the state of flow still seems overwhelming to you. In the further chapters, we will cover specific techniques to make this process as easy as possible. Likewise, you can download a short guide that will teach you a bunch of simple productivity tricks, which is available at https://simpleprogrammer. com/10hacks/.

For example, you will learn how to apply microtasks, Pomodoro timers and a Japanese Shisa Kanko procedure. All of these can be combined together to make it easy to fully immerse yourself in productive work.

How state of flow can keep you focused for a long time

While the state of flow is the most productive mental state that you can do deep work in, the amount of focus it gives you is not the only benefit of it. By its nature, the flow state can be maintained for a very long time. Far longer than the state of low-level boredom. This is because you are not wasting any energy fighting distracting thoughts. All of your mental energy is held up in the focus on the task that you are doing. Everything is working in unison.

The science that explains why the state of flow can be maintained for a long time is complicated. But we can use a simple metaphor to figure this out.

Imagine that you have 100 units of mental energy that you can spend at any one time. If you don't manage to spend it fast enough, it just replenishes itself.

Let's say you are in the state where you are trying to do deep work while actively trying to suppress any distracting thoughts. The deep work will take 50 units and it burns them slowly - at the same rate as they get replenished. So, if you didn't have a shortage of mental energy, you could, in theory, keep it up indefinitely. The only problem is that it's only 50% of your energy that is allocated to solving the problem. So you will probably not find the solution as efficiently as you could have.

But then distracting thoughts come in. And you need to spend some mental energy to get rid of them. Let's say it's 10 units per unwanted thought. But this time, those 10 units burned instantly. But the thoughts keep coming at a fast rate.

When you are shifting the focus between your work and the process of fighting distracting thoughts, you are, essentially, context-switching. And this metaphor is perhaps the best explanation of why context switching consumes so much energy.

Initially, you are fine. You have 40 more units to spend in case any new distracting thought enters your mind. But because those thoughts keep coming back at a fast rate, you quickly run out of spare energy units before you could replenish them.

Now, when the next distracting thought comes, you will have to deallocate 10 units from your actual task and allocate it to fighting this thought. So now, you find it slightly harder to focus. Your productivity takes a nosedive. Eventually, you completely run out of all mental energy units. You can no longer focus and you feel mentally drained.

Even though this is an oversimplification of the actual process, it provides a good model for what's going on. And it demonstrates why you can't keep the focus up for long when you have too many distracting thoughts in your head.

Now, imagine that you are in a state of low-level boredom. This time, you have allocated 80 units to your task. Still not optimal, but way better than previously. You will be able to work much more efficiently. And you are still burning your mental energy slowly - way slower than it can replenish itself.

Now, imagine that you still have distracting thoughts. There aren't many of them. And they aren't as strong as before. Let's say you now only need five units of mental energy to destroy each of them. But they still come in at a rate that is faster than the rate you can replenish your mental energy at.

This time, you will be able to hold on for much longer. And your focus will fade away more gradually. But it will fade away nonetheless. This is why, even though the state of low-level boredom is substantially more productive than the distracting state of overactive thought process, you still can't keep yourself in this state indefinitely. You will eventually need a break.

> Now, let's introduce the flow state. All 100 units of your mental energy are allocated to the task. And there are no distracting thoughts. None whatsoever. The parts of your brain that could have possibly generated those are completely inactive.

Disadvantages of the state of flow

At least in theory, you can keep yourself in the state of flow indefinitely. Unless some significant event brings you out of this state, you will be able to carry on working without losing your focus.

You may have experienced this yourself. Perhaps you were playing basketball and got into a state where virtually every move was perfect. You could evade your opponents. And you can score perfectly with every throw.

But then, something happened and you could no longer replicate the same level of performance in the same game. Perhaps somebody has accidentally knocked into you. Or someone managed to take the ball out of the basket at the very last moment. And that was it after that. You played the rest of the game poorly.

If you can relate to this situation - this is what demonstrates that it's usually an external situation beyond one's control that knocks us out of the state of flow. If it was up to us, we could remain in this state indefinitely.

But programming is not a contact sport. Unless you have meetings to attend and emails to answer, nothing will stop you from spending hours upon hours in the state of flow once you manage to enter it.

That's what allowed Bill Gates to spend all of his waking hours at his office when he co-founded Microsoft. And this is what made Microsoft into the tech giant it is today. That's what Bill Gates himself said about it:

"I never took a day off in my twenties. Not one." **[10]**

If you have ever heard any stories about people falling dead playing video games for several days in a row, this is most likely because they were experiencing the state of flow. Video games are actually a very good medium to induce this state. Likewise, the state of flow is the reason why musicians can play complex symphonies that last several hours.

And the fact that people can stay awake for days on end engaged in the same activity is a very good demonstration of how the state of flow works. The only way to do it is if you kind of forget about your other bodily needs. So, being in this state can actually make you not feel hunger or sleepiness. Imagine how much mental energy is available to your focus when it can be diverted even from the most basic bodily functions Akira Yasuda, a notorious game designer and the character designer for Capcom's famous arcade title Street Fighter 2, was known for his long bouts of extreme hyperfocus. This if, for example, what Tom Shirawa, one of his colleagues, said about him:

> *"He always slept under the desk. He never went back home."*

And this is what Yoshiki Okamoto, the head of arcade development at Capcom, said about him:

> *"At one point, [Yasuda] wanted to live a healthy life, so he said, "OK I'm going to drink milk." So he'd always buy these little packs of milk. He'd be working, and then he'd reach down to his little milk packs and drink them. Around his desk, he had like 100 of these packs. So he'd grab one, shake it, and whenever he'd find one with milk in it, he'd drink it and put it back, without even looking at it."*

Of course, this is an extreme example of using the state of flow. And perhaps only very few people would be capable of maintaining such hyperfocus at the expense of other life activities. But it clearly shows that achieving such a degree of hyperfocus is possible when you are in the flow.

Why state of flow will make deep work enjoyable

But the good things about the flow state don't end there. It's actually a really enjoyable state to be in. It may last indefinitely not only because you can allow it to, but also because you wouldn't want to leave it.

As a matter of fact, humans find many simple things intrinsically enjoyable. But with the amount of over-stimulation that exists all around us, many have forgotten about them. State of flow brings these feelings back, because it simply switches off all parts of your brain that aren't needed for the task that you are trying to accomplish.

Mihaly Csikszentmihalyi talks about this phenomenon in his TED talk in 2004, which is called "Flow, the secret to happiness". In fact, his whole research was motivated by the desire to find out what makes people happy rather than what makes them more productive. But while looking for one thing, he also found the other. **[5]**

And why exactly something like the state of flow can make our life enjoyable can be explained in the terms of neurochemistry. There are a number of reward chemicals our body produces that trigger good feelings that we all strive for:

- **Dopamine** is produced when we have nearly completed a meaningful task. It generates the feeling of anticipation.

- **Serotonin** is produced when we have actually accomplished something significant. It generates the feeling of happiness as a result of it.

- **Endorphins** are produced when we have done something substantial and some of our physical resources have been drained in the process. It generates pain relief and relaxation. Runner's high, for example, is caused by endorphins. **[11]**

The problem in our over-stimulated society is that the reward mechanism of our brain is constantly hijacked. We may experience a surge of dopamine while scrolling down the timeline on social media. Not only does it lead us nowhere, but it also prevents us from experiencing quiet pleasures. Those don't produce the dopamine surge as big as social media does. Therefore we stop perceiving them as something pleasurable.

Because of our modern day lifestyles, when you are trying to do any hard work, it's probably not as stimulating as your smartphone. And you will remember that. And this is why, under your normal mental state, your work will seem to be relatively boring.

Not so when you are in the state of flow. Nothing exists, but the task you are trying to accomplish. You temporarily forget that any other stimulating sources of pleasure exist. And this is how you can experience pleasure from your work.

When you are making progress - dopamine will kick in. When you have completed something - serotonin will make you feel happy. If you have to think too hard or do something physically demanding - endorphins will prevent you from over-exerting yourself and will help you to keep going.

This is why people who experience the state of flow frequently, start to deliberately seek it. It's like a drug that the brain seeks out because it wants to feel the pleasurable effects of those three key neurochemicals. And it has many of the same characteristics as being under influence does. But, unlike illicit substances, it actually enhances your life instead of destroying it.

Another thing about the state of flow is that, when the feel-good neurochemicals are released while you are in it, they are released in a balanced way. Addictive activities (like scrolling your Facebook feed) and addictive substances (like illegal drugs) work by releasing some feel-good neurochemicals but not the others. [12] Therefore, even while you feel some temporary pleasure during these activities, you still feel like something is missing. The state of flow makes you feel whole. And there is also something in us that doesn't make us feel fully happy unless we do something good for both ourselves and others. As Csikszentmihalyi said:

> *"It happens also, actually, in the most recent book I wrote, called "Good Business," where I interviewed some of the CEOs who had been nominated by their peers as being both very successful and very ethical, very socially responsible. You see that these people define success as something that helps others and at the same time makes you feel happy as you are working at it. And like all of these successful and responsible CEOs say, you can't have just one of these things be successful if you want a meaningful and successful job." [5]*

The business leaders Csikszentmihalyi has interviewed include Kenneth Derr, a former CEO and chairman of Chevron corporation, Anita Roddick, the founder of The Body Shop and Jack Greenberg, a former CEO of McDonalds.

The simplest way of getting into the state of flow

The state of flow can never be forced. In fact, if you try to force it, you will just end up in a state where you have to actively suppress many distracting thoughts. Not a good state to be in. And, as we covered in an earlier section, trying to force concentration means you will just get yourself mentally drained really fast.

Another point about the state of flow to remember is that it's not guaranteed to come. Even those who have been experiencing it on a regular basis don't experience it 100% of the time. But even if you don't manage to actually get into the state of flow, there are still some techniques that you can apply to make the process of deep work easy. We will cover them in the future chapters. But for now, here are some tips on the things you can do to try and get into the state of flow:

- The easiest way to get into the state of flow is to **just start your activity and stop thinking about the mental state itself**. It may come on its own accord in 15-20 minutes. It's not guaranteed that it will come, but with enough practice, you will be getting into this state easier.

- When you are trying to enter the state of flow, you can make things easier for yourself by using some tips commonly given to practitioners of mindfulness meditation. When some distracting thought comes, neither act upon it nor try to fight it. Simply acknowledge it in a calm and non-judgemental way and let it go. This too will be getting easier with practice.

- The choice of activity matters a lot here: **it needs to be reasonably stimulating**. This is why gamers often experience this state. And so do sportspeople and musicians, who get "in the zone".

  So, for a programmer, writing a boilerplate code or doing a basic project setup probably won't cut it. But if you need to design some system, find an annoying bug or solve a complex problem, you will be able to enter this highly coveted mental state.

- The key is to **choose a task that is neither too hard nor too easy** for you to do. If the task is too easy - you won't be able to get immersed in it. At best, you will enter a state of low-level boredom. If the task is too hard - your subconscious mind will fight against your efforts to do it. It's too energy-consuming for it. You will probably be in a very unproductive mental state with a lot of distracting thoughts.

  But when the task is just right in its complexity - it can become immersive enough to trigger the state of flow. When the problem is challenging, but is instantly perceived as solvable - your subconscious brain wouldn't mind. However, because your mind likes to conserve resources, it will switch off those parts of itself that aren't needed to solve this problem. And this is how you end up in the state of flow.

Over time, if you will practice entering this state often enough - it will become a sort of a habit. You will learn which tasks are best suited to enter this state. And you will build the right neural pathways for performing the right actions. Subconsciously, you will start performing rituals of a sort that will help you to get in the zone.

Rituals to boost productivity are what famous high-achievers are known for. For example, Jeff Bezos, the founder of Amazon, would always spend his morning doing some mindless things to allow his mind to wander and get creative. He never schedules any meetings before 10AM in the morning. [13] And here is a ritual that Scott Hanselman recommended on his Twitter to make focusing easy for those who struggle to do it while working from home:

> *"Here's a tip that my remote team does - When you get up in the morning, if you're willing and able, try COMMUTING to your home office! Go for a circle around your neighborhood and arrive back home to your home/remote office! It psychologically marks the start and end of the day." [14]*

But of course, even with years of practice, it's not guaranteed that it will happen every time. You don't control the state of flow. Your subconscious mind does. Plus, you will not always be able to do the tasks that are conducive to this state. But even then, you will build strong habits to enter the state of low-level boredom instead.

Low-level boredom is still better than your default mental state. You can still be really productive in this state. And you can still do productive deep work for substantial periods of time. So, even if you don't manage to get in the zone, you will still manage to complete your work and do so while being close to your maximum efficiency. You will still be way more productive than most. At the end of the day, very few people consciously build productive habits.

There is perhaps only one disadvantage of the flow state that you should be aware of (other than forgetting to sleep or eat or the fact that you can be jolted out of it by external factors beyond your control). Because this state is only triggered when you are performing tasks of optimal difficulty, you will, over time, need tasks of increased difficulty to trigger this state. When you spend a lot of time working on something - you eventually become good at it. And once you become a master of that activity - the activity becomes much easier.

Now, if you carry on with the same activity, you will just get bored. This is precisely why it's not uncommon for people to tell you that they fell out of love with the craft they used to enjoy. Maybe you have even experienced this yourself.

In a way, this is a good thing. At least, it's a good thing for a programming career.

When you keep mastering things of increasing difficulties just to carry on experiencing the state of flow as often as possible, you become better at what you do and have accepted the benefits and pleasure of a growth mindset and continuous life-long learning. And because you spend most of your working time doing deep work while being in the state of deep focus, you become better at what you do at the fastest rate possible.

Just remember this. And keep practicing. Keep working on harder things. You will be a master of your craft and you will never get bored with it. There are of course obstacles along the way; one of the biggest in today's world we've already briefly covered. Now let's take a deeper look at how social media is intentionally designed to make you form counter-productive habits and stand in your way.

References

1. Cal Newport - Deep Work: Rules for Focused Success in a Distracted World - Piatkus
2. Sammy Perone, Elizabeth H. Weybright and Alana J. Anderson - Over and over again: Changes in frontal EEG asymmetry across a boring task - Psychophysiology, volume 59, issue 10, October 2019
3. Dave Crenshaw - The Myth of Multitasking: How "Doing It All" Gets Nothing Done - John Wiley & Sons
4. David A. Patterson and John L. Hennessy - Computer Organization and Design: The Hardware/Software Interface. - Morgan Kaufmann
5. Mihaly Csikszentmihalyi - Flow, the secret to happiness - TED2004
6. Mihaly Csikszentmihalyi - Flow: The Psychology of Optimal Experience
7. Julia Silverstein - The Secret to Peak Performance and Optimum Focus - Entity Academy Mag, October 21, 2020
8. Amelia Hill - Boredom is good for you, study claims - The Guardian
9. https://www.hanselman.com/blog/programmings-not-for-you-how-about-thinking-be-empowered
10. Caroline Graham - This is not the way I'd imagined Bill Gates... A rare and remarkable interview with the world's second richest man - The Daily Mail, 9 June 2011
11. John Medina - Brain Rules, Updated and Expanded: 12 Principles for Surviving and Thriving at Work, Home, and School - Pear Press
12. Nir Eyal - Hooked: How to Build Habit-Forming Products - Portfolio Penguin
13. Ali Montag - This is billionaire Jeff Bezos' daily routine and it sets him up for success - CNBC, 15 September, 2018
14. https://twitter.com/shanselman

CHAPTER 3

THE FIFTH COLUMN – DETECTING AND OVERCOMING YOUR INNER SABOTEUR

I'm Not a Great Programmer, I'm Just a Good Programmer With Great Habits.
—Kent Beck

You now can fully appreciate why social media is the biggest enemy of your career as a programmer. You also know that the state of flow, the most productive mental state that you can enter, is hard to enter and to maintain. But the reason behind both of these facts is the same - we, as humans, have an inner saboteur. This inner saboteur is the thing that makes it hard for us to do the things that are in our best interests and makes it easy to do the things that don't serve us.

We, as humans, are wired in such a way that it's difficult for us to convince ourselves to do hard work. This applies even when we fully realize that this work would result in something that would benefit us. At the same time, it's difficult for us not to do something that is easy and fun when such an opportunity presents itself. And this is true even when such an action can have negative consequences, as we have discussed in chapter 1 when we talked about social media. So, when you are surrounded by quick and easy entertainment, doing hard work becomes even harder.

The good news is that it's possible to subdue this inner saboteur. And this is precisely what we will have a look at in this chapter.

But learning how to program requires hard work. But, as a programmer, you'll have to keep learning new things regularly, because technology constantly evolves and the last thing you want to do is stay behind. The programming language you know today may become obsolete tomorrow.

But if you just brute-force your way into every new programming language that you need for your job, you will soon burn out. This is where well-developed habits of effective learning will mean you constantly evolve too. And they will help you to develop the knowledge of absolutely any other technology that remains relevant and in-demand.

Likewise, in order to truly stand out as a programmer, you will need to develop a habit of discipline. And, with the right tips, it's a habit that's actually much easier to develop than it sounds. We will cover some ways you can develop it.

Once you have mastered these habits, learning anything will become easy. And your general efficiency at work will be much improved. As a bonus, you will also gain much better self-awareness.

So, let's examine what makes expert-level programming skills, seemingly reserved for the elite, so hard to develop and what meta-skills you can learn to make the hard work easy.

Why mastering programming skills requires hard work

Programming is hard. If it was easy, then anyone would have been able to do it. But only a relatively small proportion of the general population become software developers, despite a high demand for the profession.

The fact that programming is hard is precisely the reason why programmers are well-paid. In a free-market economy, your salary generally depends on three key factors - the need for what you do, your ability to do it and how difficult it is to replace you. The ability to code is in high demand and because not many people know how to program, the ones that do are hard to replace. And if, on top of this, you can do your job exceptionally well, then you can, pretty much, write your own pay-check.

Programming is not hard because of how many educational diplomas you'll have to earn. In fact, you can have none and still be a successful programmer. Many successful software developers are fully self-taught. The IT sector is probably one of the least bureaucratic industries ever. Your hiring managers would probably not care what college certificates you have. In many cases, the only thing that will be truly important to them is whether or not you can code.

But the fact that you can learn the entire set of skills just by using a computer connected to the internet doesn't make it easy. Yes, you can find all the information you need. But mastering those skills will still require hard work.

First of all, you will need to remember a lot. As a beginner, you will probably be overwhelmed with information. But this is just a tip of the iceberg. To progress in your career, you will also need to learn many different programming principles and best practices.

As a junior developer, you might get away with solving a problem any way you want. But you will never reach a more senior level unless you are familiar with design patterns, naming conventions, SOLID, KISS, DRY and other principles of clean code.

To become a truly exceptional developer, you will need to learn even more. And not just learn. You need to practice. Practice so much that you'll become a real code craftsperson.

But as every developer knows, you don't learn things only once and then just continue applying them. Technologies evolve. Programming languages get updated. With those updates, new best practices become adopted.

This is why, if you have chosen a software development career, you are in for life-long learning. And you have no choice. You can't afford not spending your time on learning and practicing new things. If you choose not to, you will soon become uncompetitive.

Learning how to program and applying this knowledge to solve actual problems requires time and focus. The time and focus that other, much more pleasant, easier, activities are always trying to take away from you.

This is why programming is incredibly hard, especially if your goal is to become a programmer that truly stands out. You may be an IT geek and programming could be the only career you have ever wanted. You may find coding enjoyable. But with unlimited access to social media, video games and streaming services, it is very hard to force yourself to actually spend your time on programming practice.

It's hard to even start doing something as mentally demanding as programming if there is a gaming console staring right at you. But it doesn't have to be this way. You can make it easy by taking advantage of the power of habits.

Why habits are the key to making hard work easy

Even though we think of ourselves as conscious creatures, the majority of the things that we do are done subconsciously. Most of the little actions we take throughout the day are done on autopilot. And that's exactly what habits are. [1]

You have probably been in a situation where you have driven somewhere and could not remember the details of the journey. Or maybe you needed to return home to check whether you have locked the door, only to discover that you have. Situations like these are good examples of how routine actions that we do every day become something that we do outside of our conscious control.

The reason why habitual actions become subconscious is that conscious thinking requires a lot of energy. According to well-established neuroscience and evolutionary biology, the brain has evolved to use this energy as efficiently as it can as part of our survival instincts. Every conscious decision we make requires a relatively high amount of energy. This is why our brain strives to automate things as much as possible.

Human brain uses up to a quarter of all the energy available to the body despite making up only approximately 2% of the total body weight. And these figures are just average for an average person. People who regularly spend a lot of time thinking hard need even more energy for their brain. [2]

The World Chess Tournament of 1984 had to be stopped abruptly. This was because one of the main contenders, Anatoly Karpov from Russia, has lost 10 kg (22 lb) of body weight and organizers were worried for his health. And all of this was caused purely by having dozens of chess matches within a relatively short period of time. This was substantial proof that heavy thinking uses so much energy that it does burn calories and can force us to use stored energy reserves. [3]

Programmers are similar to chess players in a way. Due to the nature of our work, we have to think hard too. This is why it's reasonable to assume that the work we programmers do is energy-consuming.

But according to evolutionary biology, our bodies strive to preserve as much energy as possible. We haven't evolved in an environment with surplus food, like the one we live in today. When people used to live in caves, food was scarce, so the body needed to do everything it could to preserve as much energy as possible.

This is why it's so easy to gain weight and so hard to lose it. The layer of fat is nothing but the energy store. Because even if we know exactly when our next meal is coming from, our body doesn't: Our instincts are still attuned to the harsh reality of the stone age. [4]

And exactly the same principles apply to our brains. As that incident at the chess tournament demonstrates, the process of conscious thinking can use a lot of energy. This is why, by default, our caveman instincts will do everything they can to make us do as little conscious thinking as possible.

Chances are that you have been in a situation when you needed to learn something, but you have struggled to even get started. But then, after brute-forcing the process of learning for a period of time, the activity became easier. Starting-out was hard because it was energy-consuming, but once we've done a task many times, it just becomes a subconscious habit. This is an example of this energy-preservation instinct in action.

Remember how you didn't like brushing your teeth as a kid? But over time, it just became a daily routine. You don't mind doing it. You are not asking yourself why you should do it. You just do it.

So the same can be applied to the process of mastering programming skills. You can make a routine out of it. When you start, you have to use your willpower and coerce yourself into practicing coding instead of browsing your social media feed. But if you do it consistently every day, this will become your routine.

Same applies to those who already have a successful career in software development. You may get a little complacent after your probation period is over. You may get into a habit of doing just enough not to get fired, but nowhere near enough to become a great software developer that everyone will want to hire.

Now you can use the understanding of how habits work to your advantage. You can develop routines that will gradually turn you into a person for whom complacency is virtually impossible.

Neuroscientists now know that habits physically restructure your brain. Understanding how it happens will help you to eliminate all the bad habits and build the good habits that will eventually make you into a much more productive and focused programmer.

Programmers are people with analytical minds. We like to get into details of how something works to understand it better. This is why, as a programmer, knowing how habits are formed on a biological level will make it much easier for you to start consciously applying the right habits in your own career.

Understanding the science behind habit formation

There are many things about the human brain that we still don't know. But fortunately, there is a well-established knowledge of how habits are formed. At least, all reputable neuroscientists agree on the general principles of it. [1]

If you have worked with machine learning, then you will be familiar with neural networks. But the neural networks used for machine learning are nothing more than a highly simplified mathematical model of how actual neural networks work in the brains.

Our brain consists of many neurons, which are connected to each other via a complex network. Those networks transmit signals that reach various parts of the brain. And a route in the network that the signal takes is called a neural pathway.

When we haven't done something before, we don't have any well-developed neural pathways for that action. This is why learning something completely new is always hard. The best the brain can do in this situation is re-use some neural pathways that are vaguely related to the action we are trying to do. This may allow us to complete the action, but our performance will be abysmal, and the energy consumed will be high.

A model has been developed by psychologists that describe four stages of competence that a person goes through while learning something new. [5] Those are as follows:

- Unconscious incompetence. In programming, this is when a programmer hasn't yet started learning a new technology that he or she needs for the job and can't possibly appreciate how difficult this technology is to master.

- Conscious incompetence. This is when a programmer has already started learning a specific technology and fully realizes what gaps of knowledge he or she has.

- Conscious competence. This is when a programmer can use the technology well, but needs to apply conscious focus every time he or she uses it.

- Unconscious competence. This is when a programmer has mastered a particular technology to such a level that it can be applied on autopilot.

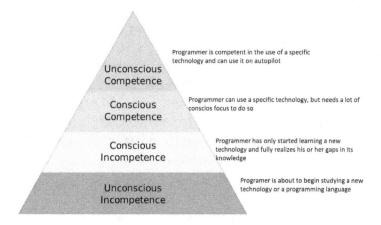

Unconscious
Competence

Programmer is competent in the use of a specific technology and can use it on autopilot

Conscious
Competence

Programmer can use a specific technology, but needs a lot of conscios focus to do so

Conscious
Incompetence

Programmer has only started learning a new technology and fully realizes his or her gaps in its knowledge

Unconscious
Incompetence

Programer is about to begin studying a new technology or a programming language

The four stages of competence

Remember when you used the computer keyboard for the first time? Or when you've taken your first driving lesson? You were probably able to follow the instructions, but it took you a long time to type that first word or to drive the first 20 yards.

When we do something repeatedly, the neural pathways associated with that physical action become stronger. A new highway gets built in the network of neurons inside our brain. And then it becomes really easy for neurons to fire. This is why, over time, you are able to type on a computer or drive a car without even thinking about it. The energy-reserving brain likes this because forging new pathways is hard. **[6]**

As Daniel J. Siegel, a famous psychiatrist and an author, said: *"Where attention goes, neural firing flows, and neural connection grows."*. *[7]*

But this principle is not only limited to the process of learning new skills. This applies to establishing new routines too. Neural pathways don't just control the physical actions your body can take. Cues and associations are also transmitted by neurons as signals.

For example, there isn't much skill involved in brushing your teeth. It's a series of very simple moves that even a little kid can do without any effort. Only that the kid will probably find the process unnecessary, boring and time-consuming.

But over time, the process of brushing teeth just becomes a routine. Your brain would have built a neural pathway based on cues. It might be that your brain associates getting up from your bed as a cue for brushing teeth. Or maybe it's the sound of the alarm clock. Whichever exact association it is, when the morning comes, you just go to the bathroom and start brushing your teeth. And you aren't even thinking of it. You don't remember what exact hand movements you've made when you brushed your teeth last time, do you? And that's because the action was fully subconscious.

Now, you know how habits are formed on the biological level. This will now help you to deal with the process that is perhaps the most destructive to your programming career - procrastination.

Why we procrastinate

As a software developer, you will have to regularly deal with the urge to procrastinate. And you'll find it hard to resist, especially when there are so many distractions around you.

But if you want to be a truly exceptional programmer, procrastination is your mortal enemy. Every hour you spend procrastinating is an hour you could have spent developing your professional skills, but didn't. The more you procrastinate - the more you are putting your professional development on hold.

It may be even worse. Procrastination may delay you when you try to complete an urgent piece of work. And if this was a mission-critical task that had to be completed before a strict deadline, you may even get fired for that.

And procrastination is not even pleasant. You gain absolutely nothing from it. Remember last time you were meant to complete a task, but ended up mindlessly browsing the web instead? If you are like me, then you have probably felt guilty about not completing your task, while the process of browsing the web didn't give you any real pleasure either.

So why then do we procrastinate, if there are no benefits from it whatsoever, while it also harms your career progress?

You now know that the brain is an energy-consuming organ that likes to preserve the energy as much as it can. And this is the primary reason why we procrastinate.

If the brain perceives the task at hand to be too difficult, it will try its best to make you avoid it. This is why, even if you fully understand the benefits of doing the work, there will be some sort of subconscious urge to make you do something else instead. Normally, you will have a craving to do something much less difficult and much more pleasant. This is why when you procrastinate, you normally end up doing some mindless things, like continuously scrolling your social media feed or binge-watching YouTube videos.

It is a form of self-sabotage. But your subconscious mind doesn't perceive it as such. According to it, it's trying to save you from potentially using up too many resources. Remember that your subconscious mind still lives in the stone age where your next meal wasn't guaranteed. [8]

And any task that you haven't done before will be especially prone to be perceived by your brain as something too big and too hard. It doesn't yet have anything it can compare the difficulty of this task with. So, by default, it will just put it into the category of "too big".

Procrastination can be an easy trap to fall into for anyone, but it's especially a problem for anyone involved in intellectually challenging work, including software developers.

As a software developer, you will regularly do something that you haven't done before. Sometimes you will be learning a new technology. Sometimes you will be investigating a problem in a system that you aren't too familiar with. If you can't estimate how challenging the task will be, by default, your brain will perceive it as too difficult. There is no getting away from it. It's how the brain works on the basic biological level.

And you can probably relate to it yourself. Do you remember the inner resistance that you have felt when you needed to study a new technology or a programming language? Or maybe you felt it when you needed to build a feature or investigate a bug in a system that you aren't very familiar with? Perhaps you have been putting it off for as long as you could. But then, once you get started, it doesn't feel that bad anymore and you are fairly happy to continue.

The fact that experiencing the urge to procrastinate is sometimes inevitable doesn't mean that you can't fight that urge and win. This is exactly what habits are for. Procrastination is a habit. The more you succumb to the urge to procrastinate - the harder it will be to resist it in the future.

But successfully convincing yourself to get the work done despite the urge to procrastinate can also become a habit. You just need to do it frequently enough. Over time, you will be able to resist this urge easily.

Now, let's talk about more concrete steps on developing productivity habits.

How to make coding as easy as brushing your teeth

If you have good oral hygiene, then the process of brushing your teeth will be second nature to you. But to be an extraordinary software developer, you will need to make your technical skills second nature too.

You already know how neural pathways form and why it's so hard for software developers not to procrastinate. And, of course, programming is not even comparable to brushing your teeth. It is way more difficult.

Well, the bad news is that once you make a decision to become a master of the software development craft, you will have to overcome some serious obstacles. You will have no choice in this matter. You will have to use your willpower.

But the good news is that you will only do so at the beginning. Once new neural pathways are formed and solidified, your work will feel easy. Your subconscious mind will know exactly how difficult each task will be if it's similar to the ones you've done many times before and you will no longer feel an urge to procrastinate. Or maybe you still feel the urge, but it won't be so strong that you won't be able to deal with it.

And this is where the analogy of brushing teeth comes into play. You probably no longer brush your teeth because you are actively worried about your oral hygiene. You brush your teeth because, over the years, you have built many cues that make you go and brush your teeth.

The same principles can be applied to building good working habits. If you feel your environment with certain cues, then, over time, your subconscious will start associating these cues with work. And you will be able to give your work 100% focus.

It can be anything. Different techniques will have a different degree of success for different people. But the general principles will apply to everyone.

Scott Hanselman, one of the most famous senior software developers from Microsoft, seems to be a genius of productivity. He blogs. He films videos. He interviews people. He travels around the world and gives talks. He publishes programming courses. And this is on top of his already busy work at Microsoft. And, on top of that, he has a family.

But he isn't actually that special. One of the most popular themes of his talks is productivity hacks. And when you listen to those, it appears to be that he is just extremely good at designing routines. And his routines become solid habits. [9]

Basically, as well as being a true master of software development, he is also a master of meta-skills. But he doesn't keep it a secret that it's precisely the meta-skills that made him a successful software developer and not the other way round.

For example, he talks a lot about setting up a distraction-free environment and making it a habit to focus only on a narrow range of things that are required to achieve a specific goal.

He is also really good at not letting his professional work interfere with his private life. And his routine allows him sufficient opportunities to recharge. For example, he completely switches off his devices when he is around his family in the evenings, on the weekends or during their vacations. [10]

Here, Scott Hanselman has shown us one of the greatest habit-forming techniques you can use. You can separate your work from other aspects of your life and create strong associative cues to make your work much more focused and productive.

You can separate your work from other parts of your life by time, space or both. For example, you could:

- Have a special alarm ring-tone that will indicate the start of the work time.

- Always start your work at exactly the same time.

- Do your work in a special room that exists only for work.

- Keep your working computer just for work and nothing else.

You can choose whatever works best for you. Later, we will cover in more detail why these routines work, so you will better understand how to design your own routine for enhanced productivity.

But for the time being, just remember that consistency is the key. If you carry on performing these little rituals while you work, your brain will start to associate them with work. And over time, you will get to the state where a particular cue will make you sit down and start working without giving it a second thought.

If you haven't been consciously working on your productivity before, the initial period will probably be challenging. Most people are like this. And to them, some days that can focus, while on other days they get hardly anything done.

What you need to start doing is forcing yourself to start doing the work, even if you don't feel like it. To make it easy, you can associate cues with it. Maybe you can try to do it every day at a particular time. Maybe it will always be at a particular place. Maybe you will do it on a device that you have been using for work and nothing else. Or maybe it's a combination of those.

What you do repeatedly becomes your subconscious habit. And this is how you build a habit of jumping into a productive activity when you see certain cues. You just continue doing it over and over again in the same way until you start doing it on autopilot.

Over time, the tasks themselves will become easier. If you regularly study new material, you will learn how to enjoy the process. If you write code regularly and frequently, many of the programming techniques will become second nature to you. Once you have experienced a repeated exposure to finding and fixing bugs, you will know exactly where to look when you'll be working with similar systems. Your brain will no longer perceive those as particularly challenging tasks.

But to make coding a second nature, you have to do a lot of it. You have no choice. Habits take time to form. And repetition is the key.

What exact habits successful programmers have

Martin Fowler, who is well-known in the software industry as probably the main expert on software design and architecture, frequently uses this famous quote from Kent Beck, to emphasize how much of his career success is attributed to habits: *"I'm not a great programmer; I'm just a good programmer with great habits."*

But what exact habits do you need to develop to become a great programmer? Well, the most fundamental habits that you need to work on are the ones that apply to any field, not just programming. Let's call them "the habits of discipline".

But, contrary to a popular misconception, discipline is not entirely about using your willpower to do difficult things even when you don't want to do them. Discipline is also about restructuring your environment and your routine in such a way that it would make it easy to do those things that would help you achieve your goals. With those changes in places, you won't have to use a lot of willpower.

And one of the best changes you can apply to your working environment as a programmer is to reduce the amount of cognitive load in it.

How to reduce cognitive load

Those are the habits that will allow you to keep focused on useful tasks. Until you develop those, you will have to exert willpower. And as we have already determined, willpower (which is the same as consciously maintaining focus on something that you don't want to do) is a finite resource. It consumes energy, which is finite, until you do something to replenish it.

But the things that replenish energy usually take a lot more time than the things that deplete it. This is why people need eight hours of sleep on average, while most of them can only maintain conscious focused activity for a couple of hours per day at most.

One of the things that gets you tired the most during challenging cognitive work, like software development, is the process of deciding to do the work. It's not as simple as just making the decision to do the work and immediately sitting down to do it. Because the task you are about to do competes with a whole range of various pleasant activities you could do instead, the process of making such a decision includes conscious or semiconscious assessment of pros and cons of doing the task compared to other things you crave to do instead. This is why it's so exhausting.

The process of getting exhausted from making too many conscious decisions is known as decision fatigue or ego depletion. The term "ego depletion" was first coined by Roy Baumeister - a world-class social psychologist. Since then, a lot of research has been done on the subject. [11]

Some successful entrepreneurs just understood this concept intuitively. Steve Jobs, for example, used to wear exactly the same outfit all the time. He just had several exact copies of it in his wardrobe. But this was just one of the best-known rituals to minimize the decision fatigue that he did. He had several of those. For example, he was notorious for saying "no" to almost every idea that came his way and he aggressively delegated tasks. [12]

Even though the process of selecting what to wear is seemingly easy, it does deplete your mental energy a little bit. And if you have to make many little decisions like this, all of these small energy depletions add up. So, if you manage the number of decisions you have to routinely make to an absolute minimum, then you will have sufficient energy to make really hard decisions, which he, as Apple CEO, had to make many of on a regular basis.

So, you need to build a habit of doing focused work without thinking about more pleasant things that you would prefer to do instead. And for that, you will need to minimize ego depletion.

A good trick would be to eliminate as many distracting cues from your environment as possible. Then the habit will solidify much quicker.

It will probably be hard for you to focus on your work if you are a gamer and there is a poster of your favorite game in the room you are trying to do your work in. Or even worse - when there is an actual gaming console right next to your desk. If you use social media a lot - it will be hard to resist the temptation to scroll through your timeline when you are logged into your profile on the computer you are trying to work on.

So, clear any logins to the entertainment resources you have on your work computer's browser. Uninstall all the entertainment apps and games from it. Put your phone on silent and move it out of your sight. Or better yet, move it into a different room.

You can go full Steve Jobs by throwing away the entire content of your wardrobe and buying multiple copies of exactly the same outfit. This would be helpful. But for the vast majority of people, this would be an overkill.

As you can now see, the most effective way of improving your discipline is not by forcing yourself to do hard things, but to rearrange your environment in such a way that it would be easy to do those things. If your environment helps you to focus on your productive work, then you won't have to apply too much willpower to maintain your focus. And if you constantly keep removing cognitive clutter from your environment, you will become disciplined without having to force yourself.

Developing good programming habits

As well as mastering the fundamental habits of discipline, you obviously need to develop good programming habits. And it's not only about being able to type the code intuitively. This is probably the least important thing, although you will gain this skill after typing a lot of code over a long period of time.

What you need to work on is mastering the habits of doing software development in a proper way. You need to make it a second nature to write clean code, well-maintainable and bug-free code and not just any code.

Martin Fowler gives this timeless advice to help us develop good programming habits: [13]

> *"If you can get today's work done today, but you do it in such a way that you can't possibly get tomorrow's work done tomorrow, then you lose."*

> *"When you find you have to add a feature to a program, and the program's code is not structured in a convenient way to add the feature, first refactor the program to make it easy to add the feature, then add the feature"*

These practices that he has developed over the decades is exactly what sets him apart from someone who has been coding for an equivalent amount of time, but has never learned to do it well.

And those quotes just summarize the purpose of structuring your code properly instead of just writing any random bunch of statements. Best practices, such as SOLID principles, coding style conventions and design patterns are there for a reason. Yes, you can write code that solves any particular problem without applying any of these best practices and if your code ends up badly structured as the result, you will cause yourself a bunch of problems in the future.

This is precisely why badly written code is referred to as "technical debt". Yes, you may save a little bit of time right now by writing a solution to a specific problem without taking a step back and thinking about the best practices. But this negligible amount of time saved will result in significantly more work in the future when you will have no choice but to restructure a badly written code. This is precisely why Martin Fowler says that it's worth refactoring badly written code every time when you see it. This little amount of extra work now will save you a lot of hassle in the future.

So, what specific best practices do you need to implement? Well, there are plenty of those and you won't remember them all. And you don't need to know them all right away anyway. SOLID, KISS and DRY principles are examples of these best practices, along with above mentioned coding style conventions and design patterns. But covering them in detail is beyond the scope of our subject.

To develop the habit of applying best practices while writing software, the easiest thing you can do is spend some time each week reading books and blogs written by well-respected software developers to find out the details of those best practices, make notes of the key concepts and then start incorporating them into your code. Over time, your code will become better and better. And those best practices will be something that you do completely intuitively.

Dedicating a specific time frame on a specific day of the week to learning best practices will help you to establish a consistent routine, which itself will eventually become a habit. This kind of approach to productivity is what Scott Hanselman advocates and regularly mentions in his blog and his talks.

It's important to remember that merely knowing the syntax of a programming language is not enough. In order to be a good software developer, you need to know how to use this language well. And it's those best practices that prescribe it. So, in order to be a true master of your craft, make those best practices your habit.

Why soft skills are also important

But to become a truly exceptional software developer, mastering software craftsmanship is not enough. You will also need to obtain reasonably good soft skills. These include a whole range of interpersonal skills, like communication, leadership, the ability to sell, etc..

Of course, you aren't a professional public speaker (although nobody is saying you can't be one). And you aren't a salesperson either (although we all have to sell something from time to time; we just don't tend to call it that). So perhaps you don't need to develop your soft skills to a level where you can win a political debate against a professional politician. But nevertheless, if you want to be successful in your career, any career for that matter, you have to at least develop the following skills to a fairly good level:

- Your salary doesn't only depend on how good you are as a coder. Many people wish it did, but it isn't how things work in real life. Your salary also depends on your ability to **negotiate**.

- Not all good jobs are accessible via just a resume. In fact, when you look at top-level jobs, probably only a small fraction of those are obtained by a standard application process. More often, you will get a job offer based on how you present yourself as a professional. For example, some directors may have liked the way you presented yourself at some conference. Or maybe some hiring manager saw your blog and really liked it.

- If you don't have good **communication** skills, you won't get far, even if your technical skills are exceptional. If you are the best coder in the company but nobody wants to work with you, you won't get promoted. If your idea is objectively the best, but you can't sell it at a meeting, your idea won't get implemented.

- Lastly, almost any well-paid high-level role in almost any industry consists of **leadership** components. Senior software developers no longer just code. They influence their teams. So, without even the minimal ability to influence, you won't be able to become a senior software developer.

But the approach towards learning soft skills and making them your habits is similar to mastering hard technical skills. Dedicate some time to learning them and then consciously try to adjust your behavior and the way you talk according to what you have learned.

Over time, even if you won't become completely charismatic, you will at least become someone that is pleasant to work with and who can influence other people. Your ideas will actually get implemented, because you will be able to present them well. And you may even receive a job offer out of the blue because someone really liked something you said.

I am personally acquainted with these principles. I used to be fairly shy and introverted in the past. I wasn't much of a communicator. And I did think that success in a software development career should be driven purely by technical merit.

Until I changed my attitude, I was stuck in a mid-level position. But since I started proactively working on my soft skills, my career has improved dramatically.

One thing that I did was to start blogging and filming video lectures about programming. Since then, I have received a number of job offers from good reputable companies purely because someone found my blog or one of my lectures.

And working on my face-to-face interactions has also played a positive role in my career. I got hired into a lead software engineer position because I've made friends with someone who later obtained a top managerial position.

So, while technical skills are extremely important for the development of your programming career, you will quickly hit the limit unless you also work on your soft skills.

But as well as building good habits, you absolutely need to make sure that you don't allow bad habits to form and solidify. Those can easily derail you, even if you have already established some good habits.

How to stop bad habits sabotaging your progress

One of the most important things to remember about habits is that the process of habit-formation doesn't only build positive habits. It builds any habits, including destructive ones. This is why, as well as deliberately working towards building the habits that will help you to achieve your goals, you must always be on the lookout for the habits that can sabotage your progress.

Unlike positive habits, negative habits are never in the open. You don't have to think about them. They will just form on their own. This is why you need to pay attention to the actions that you do throughout the day. [14]

Another feature of negative habits is that they take no effort at all. Those are the habits that will form by default if you don't take any conscious action to develop yourself into the person you want to be.

There are many negative habits that everyone is aware of - over-eating, binge-drinking and smoking. Those are bad for your health. And they can also turn into full-blown addictions. But there are also some nasty habits that are perhaps less known and more socially acceptable that can, nevertheless, derail your career.

Procrastination, that we have already been talking about, is one of them. As with any other harmful habits, you don't need to put any effort into building it. The inclination to procrastinate is what you will naturally feel from time to time. And if you succumb to it too many times, it will become a strongly ingrained habit that will become extremely difficult to get rid of.

So does the habit of ignoring best practices when you write your code. It's much easier to just write the code than also thinking about how to structure it properly. But overtime, this habit may turn your codebase into an unmaintainable mess. And it may also cost your professional reputation and your career. You may become known as someone who writes junk code despite the years of experience. And if this happens, nobody would want to hire you.

The best time to get rid of any destructive habit is when it hasn't yet developed into a fully blown habit. Your brain wouldn't have built strong enough neural pathways at that point. Once it does, it will take a lot of time and effort to weaken those neural pathways.

And this is why, if your goal is to be as successful as you can possibly be in your career, you need to build one particular habit - a habit to regularly examine your thoughts and actions throughout the day. Only this way you will be able to spot the patterns of your behavior that may, over time, develop into a habit that you don't want to have.

Using mindfulness to stop bad habits forming

There are many ways you can achieve it. Mindfulness meditation is one of the most popular ways. There are several different ways of doing it, but the most basic method is to sit in a comfortable position with your eyes closed and pay attention to your breath. Every time you notice some thoughts - you must refocus your attention on your breath.

Jon Kabat-Zinn, a mindfulness expert and a founder of Stress Reduction Clinic has said the following: *"Mindfulness means being awake. It means knowing what you are doing."* **[15]**

The main benefit of mindfulness is precisely that - knowing what you are doing. Getting to know those things about yourself that you don't normally pay much attention to. And this is precisely why mindfulness is one of the best ways of spotting your hidden bad habits that are trying to creep in and become ingrained.

If you do the meditation regularly for 10 to 30 minutes, then you will gain better awareness of your thought patterns. This will help you spot any thoughts that can potentially build negative habits. Once you notice those, you can take appropriate action to eliminate them.

Spotting bad habits through journaling

But sitting down quietly with your eyes closed won't suit everyone. If meditation is not your thing, there are plenty of other techniques you can employ to examine your behavior. For example, you can get into the habit of journaling. When you are about to go to bed, you can write down what happened during your day, paying particular attention to your actions. As well as writing down any actions you are proud of, you need to write the ones you aren't proud of that much.

Markus Aurelius, one of the best-known Roman emperors and one of the most famous practitioners of Stoicism, performed journaling regularly. And this perhaps was one of the main things that helped him to maintain the upstanding character he was known for. In fact, his book "Meditation" that every practicing Stoic has read is nothing more than a collection of his journal entries. [16]

When you put your thoughts on paper, you remember them better. Therefore, over time, your journal will show you your behavior patterns that you probably should change.

Replacing bad habits with good habits

But what to do if you spot a negative habit forming? The best thing you can do is replace it with a good habit. So, if you are feeling a slight urge to procrastinate - shift your attention to something productive. Then, immediately performed this productive action. Over time, your thought about procrastination will become a cue for such an action.

But why is it that the best way to eliminate a bad habit is to replace it with a good one? Again, we are going back to the biology of our brain. When you build a good habit to replace a bad one, you build one neural pathway to weaken the other one.

When neural pathways form, neurons have to establish new connections. And if those connections are used frequently, they become stronger. On the other hand, the connections that aren't used as much become weaker.

The reason why you can eliminate the procrastination habit by shifting your attention towards productive work is because you are redirecting your neural network away from the existing cue. The action of shifting focus, if regularly done, will contribute towards a new neural pathway. And, over time, the mere thought about procrastination will make you automatically shift your focus to something productive. You'll do it unconsciously. There'll be a well-used neural pathway for that.

But whether you are building good habits or trying to eliminate bad ones - always remember that habit formation takes time.

Why you should not be discouraged if things remain hard for a while

Consistently building productive habits while eliminating unproductive ones is the best and the easiest way of building yourself into a person you want to be. But nothing worthwhile is easy in the absolute terms. Therefore it will probably still take you a while to build those necessary habits.

When focusing during your work or study isn't getting easier over time - don't be discouraged. It's meant to be this way.

How long and how easy it will be depends on how many habits you have already developed and whether it's the good or the bad habits that dominate. So, if programming is harder for you than it is for your peers, it doesn't necessarily mean that you aren't as good as them. It may mean that you simply carry more counter-productive baggage in your brain than they do.

You don't have to be a genius to be an exceptional programmer that everybody wants to hire. What you do need is the ability to focus and to foster the other good habits we've discussed. What will set you apart is the ability to focus.

We are all different. A young person with no experience whatsoever can pick up programming really easily. Such a person wouldn't have had any strongly ingrained habits yet. The neural network inside their brain would still be fresh. This is why you can just mold it into anything.

A person with a whole range of unproductive habits will find it hard to become productive. By trying to build new productive habits, this person will be building neural pathways that will compete with many strong and well-established pathways that exist already. This is a person that will probably require a lot of time and willpower to turn into someone successful.

You may also know someone who has been highly productive their whole life. For example, a successful research scientist may want to decide to become a software developer. In this case, chances are that such a person will become a fully competent programmer in a much shorter time than an average computer science graduate.

This is because such a person would have already built a strong set of base habits that are transferable to any other scientific or engineering discipline. The neural network inside their brain is already correctly configured. And this is why there are many successful software developers who are self-taught. And many of them come from engineering or science backgrounds.

This process can be observed in religious Jewish families, where people tend to become more financially successful than average, even under the most unfavorable of the circumstances. For example, despite arriving in the US in the early 20th century with virtually nothing, the vast majority of people from Jewish background were able to establish successful businesses and build successful careers. [17]

The reason for this is that the Jewish tradition dictates that children need to study a lot. And they are mandated to read complex religious texts.

Not everyone remains religious when they grow up. But the learning skills they have obtained as kids remain with them for the rest of their lives. And this is how they can then learn almost any in-demand skills.

If you aren't getting anywhere, it's OK. Every positive action contributes towards building a positive habit. Every time you don't give in to a distracting thought that has been driven by a bad habit builds your habit of not giving in to distracting thoughts. You just need to keep building the right habits.

You may not have come from a background of education. And perhaps you have accumulated many negative habits throughout your life. But this doesn't mean that you can't become truly successful. This merely means that the process of transforming yourself may take a little bit longer.

Don't compare yourself to somebody else. Instead, compare yourself to the person you were yesterday.

Trust the process. The results will come.

A metaphor that will help you to remember how habits work

Imagine your mind as your garden. What happens to your garden if you don't look after it? It gets overgrown with weeds.

Weeds don't require any help from you. And they will sprout up in the least expected places.

If a garden weed is still small, it won't do much damage. And you can pull it out easily.

But if the weed is already fully grown, it can do a lot of damage. It can poison your soil, so your garden plants can no longer grow there. And if you try to pull it out, you will probably cause some damage. Or maybe you won't be able to pull it out at all if the root system is too big.

Garden plants, on the other hand, require a lot of effort. If you don't get soil chemistry correctly, they may die. If you don't water them enough, they may die. Or maybe they won't die, but they won't grow the way you want them to grow.

And the more beautiful a garden plant is - the more active maintenance it requires.

A weed represents a habit that forms on its own. It will form without any effort from your side. And while it's still in its infancy, you can eliminate it easily. When it grows to a certain size, it may start causing damage. And it will then become difficult, if not impossible, to get rid of it.

The garden plants are like your positive habits. You have to actively maintain them. If you won't - they will die. Or maybe they will grow into something nasty. For example, persistence is a good habit. But it can become bad if you are persistent in doing something counterproductive.

The most precious and beautiful garden plants are like the habits of excellence. They are the ones that truly set you above everyone else. And they are the ones that require the most maintenance.

Gardening work is hard, especially if you want to build a truly beautiful garden. But so is building the right habits to become an exceptional programmer. But if you want to have a career that can be compared to a beautiful garden - the work is absolutely necessary.

You can however make this process a little easier by following some of my productivity hacks, at https://simpleprogrammer.com/10hacks/

You now know why building the right habits and the ability to do deep work are very important for building a successful career as a programmer. You now also know how modern smart technology, especially social media, can act as a significant obstacle on the way of your career success.

But just following the right habits, doing deep work and exercising digital minimalism is not enough. Unless you also develop the right mindset, all of these will seem to you as unnecessary chores.

So, in the next section we will talk about building the right mindset for becoming a successful software developer. And we will start with the importance of putting yourself inside a social environment of the right kind - the so-called "echo-chamber".

References

1. Dr. Mike Dow - Your Subconscious Brain Can Change Your Life: Overcome Obstacles, Heal Your Body, and Reach Any Goal with a Revolutionary Technique - Hay House Inc
2. Michael W. Richardson - How Much Energy Does the Brain Use? - brainfacts.org
3. J. Spearman and Jon Tisdal - Moscow Marathon: World Chess Championship, 1984-85 - HarperCollins Publishers Ltd
4. James G. Ferry and Christopher H. House - The Stepwise Evolution of Early Life Driven by Energy Conservation - Molecular Biology and Evolution, Volume 23, Issue 6, June 2006
5. Broadwell, Martin M. (20 February 1969). "Teaching for learning (XVI)". wordsfitlyspoken.org. The Gospel Guardian. Retrieved 11 May 2018.

6. Benjamin Gardner and Amanda L. Rebar - Habit Formation and Behavior Change - Oxford Research Encyclopaedias
7. Daniel J. Sieagel - Aware: The Science and Practice of Presence - TarcherPerigree
8. Jane B. Burka and Lenora M. Yuen - Procrastination: Why You Do It, What to Do About It Now - Da Capo Lifelong Books
9. Scott Hanselman - Scott Hanselman's Complete List of Productivity Tips - https://www.hanselman.com
10. Scott Hanselman - This developer's life 1.1.0 - Disconnecting. https://www.hanselman.com/blog/this-developers-life-110-disconnecting
11. Roy F. Baumeister - Willpower: Rediscovering the Greatest Human Strength - Penguin Random House USA
12. Waater Isaacson - Steve Jobs
13. https://martinfowler.com/
14. Wendy Wood - Good Habits, Bad Habits: The Science of Making Positive Changes - Macmillan USA
15. Jon Kabat-Zinn - Wherever You Go, There You Are: Mindfulness meditation for everyday life - Piatkus
16. Marcus Aurelius - Meditations
17. Amy Chua - The Triple Package: How Three Unlikely Traits Explain the Rise and Fall of Cultural Groups in America - Penguin Books

CHAPTER 4

HOW ECHO-CHAMBERS CAN HELP YOU IN YOUR CAREER

You're the average of five people you spend the most time with.

—*Jim Rohn*

You already know the importance of building the right habits if you want to become an elite-level software developer. If you don't consciously work on your habits, you can still be a good developer, but you will never be truly exceptional.

By now, you can appreciate how critical is the ability to do deep work in an intellectually-challenging profession like programming. Without it, you won't be able to solve complex problems and deliver the results quickly, as only elite-level programmers can. And deep work is just another habit, which, if mastered, will allow you to enter a truly productive mental state, known as the state of flow.

And you know that nothing else can be as damaging to both building the right habits and being able to do deep work as social media. It was deliberately designed to monopolize your attention and distract you from your own goals. And it has very powerful mechanisms to do so.

We haven't focused on any specific technical skills that are needed to become an elite-level software developer. Instead, we talked about the things you can do to build yourself into a kind of a person for whom the tasks of learning any required technical skills and applying those skills in the real world is easy.

And the specific part that we have focused on was related to building the habits that are helpful to your goals, while preventing yourself from unconsciously acquiring any negative habits that could potentially derail your goals.

Habits are critically important. But they are only one part of this equation. The other critically important part is the mindset.

It's a growth mindset that provides you with the intrinsic motivation to achieve your goals. It's a growth mindset that makes you deliberately work on your habits, even when you don't feel like it.

A growth mindset is what generates that inner voice that reminds you why you shouldn't be satisfied with just any type of mediocre job that provides you with bare necessities. It's the same inner voice that tells you why you shouldn't just spend all your evenings sitting in front of the TV with a six-pack of beer and a slice of pizza.

Habits provide you the means of achieving your goals or anything extraordinary in life. But that habit formation requires work, and it's the growth mindset that gives you the reason why you need to do that work; to achieve your goals and move beyond being content with what you already have.

Echo-chambers are one way to cultivate and build-up a strong growth mindset. Even if in the past you've struggled with levels of motivation and ambition, an echo-chamber can help mold your mindset into one where you believe you can be a high-achiever and you feel a strong desire to do everything you can to make it so.

What is mindset?

I use the word "mindset" here as an all-encompassing term that includes your core beliefs, attitude towards things, personal principles (which you will not be willing to violate), life philosophy, and your character.

In a way, mindset is also a habit. Your core beliefs form when you keep seeing the confirmation of how certain things work over and over again, until you start to operate while being 100% convinced that those ideas are true. Your attitude is formed by your experience.

The personal principles get formed from your experience too and the ability to consistently adhere to them comes with practice. Over time, your life experience solidifies into your personal philosophy. And this is how your overall character is built. **[1]**

But unlike any other types of habits that you can develop on your own, mindset doesn't form in a vacuum. Our mindset depends on the feedback we constantly receive from our environment. And that primarily includes the people you interact with, either directly or indirectly.

It doesn't matter how much you want to believe that any particular thing is true. If you don't have any feedback from your environment that confirms it - you will never be able to convince yourself that it's true. And it will never become your core belief: a part of your mindset.

If you aspire to become a great software developer but you don't personally know anyone who is one - it will be very hard to convince yourself that a person like you can ever achieve the elite level. By default, your mind will start coming up with excuses for why those extraordinary programmers you've read about are special cases and why the way they achieved their success would never be applicable to you. **[2]**

When someone believes in something, it's rarely because it's an objective fact. Most often, it's because they have received enough feedback from their environment to confirm this idea, even if what their mind has perceived as a valid confirmation is nothing more than a cognitive bias. **[3]**

Cognitive biases are not necessarily bad. After all, if they weren't helpful, they wouldn't have survived the process of evolution. It's OK to have beliefs that are somewhat unrealistic, as long as those beliefs serve you in the process of achieving your goals.

For example, if you are fully convinced that becoming a millionaire is something that you can achieve if you put enough effort into it, you may still not become a millionaire. But, nevertheless, the actions that you would have taken will probably get you to earn a comfortable six-figure annual income.

On the other hand, if you don't believe that you are someone who can become a millionaire and that only the lucky few ever do, you may still be able to try. But this time, you will really have to force yourself to. After all, if people become millionaires purely out of luck and your effort doesn't matter, to your subconscious mind those actions you are trying to take will seem like an unnecessary waste of resources.

Also, the subconscious mind really doesn't like cognitive dissonances. It doesn't like to be proven wrong when you have programmed it to be convinced of something. Therefore it will subtly sabotage your efforts, just so you can say to yourself: "see, I told you that becoming a millionaire is impossible". [4]

This is why it's much more important to have core beliefs that serve you rather than the ones that are objectively true. Statistically speaking, the belief that you won't ever become a millionaire is probably more realistic than the alternative. But it's the belief that you can achieve that level of wealth that will almost certainly help you to build a great life for yourself, even if the end-goal of becoming an actual millionaire is never achieved.

Because mindset is so important, as well as adjusting your everyday actions, you will also need to make adjustments to the environment you spend most of your time in. You need to configure it in such a way that it gives you the type of feedback that helps you cultivate a growth mindset and achieve your goals. And perhaps the most important adjustment that you can make is deliberately choosing the group of people you spend most of the time with.

Why your mindset depends on who you regularly talk to

You might have heard a cliche that you are an average of five people you spend most time with. This is perhaps not 100% accurate, but it still provides a good model of how things actually work.

Of course, you will never lose your original personality just by being a member of a certain group of people. That is, unless you join a cult. Cults are designed to erase everything that makes you unique, so you can become an obedient pawn in a cult leader's game. But still, your personality will be affected by people around you.

When we interact with people, we subconsciously absorb their ideas. Our brains have mirror neurons and we have evolved to get into rapport with those around us, especially the ones we spend most of our time with. **[5]**

Mirror neurons are the brain's way of making us fit in a group of people. This was an important survival mechanism, as for our stone age predecessors being exiled from the group would almost guarantee death. This is why humans aren't naturally solitary. And this is why our brains would make us subconsciously adjust our behavior via the mirror neurons to be more like people we interact with the most.

And this absorption of ideas does not distinguish between good or bad ideas. If a particular idea is widely accepted in a particular group, this is what most of the group members will probably accept. From the standpoint of our brain, belonging in the group is more important than having the right idea. It's due to the fact that, back in the stone age, being the smartest person in the tribe wouldn't give you any advantage if you were exiled from the group to fend on your own.

And we should never underestimate how many limitations people in our surrounding can instill in us, even without knowing. For example, there is a theory in psychology known as "crab mentality". It originated as a metaphor that describes what happens when you put crabs in a bucket. **[6]**

When you place one crab in a bucket and leave it, it will just crawl out. However, when you place many crabs in a bucket, none of them escape. All the crabs will try to escape at the same time and, by doing so, they will end up pulling each other back down.

The same thing happens in human society. When people try to achieve something that is atypical of people within their surrounding, they often get dissuaded from doing so, either deliberately or unconsciously. They get "pulled back down" in a metaphorical way.

When everyone in your environment smokes, it will be extremely hard to give up, even if you really want to. You may be able to go cold-turkey without any difficulties, but only until you'll meet your friends again and all of them will start lighting up in front of you.

If all you do with your friends is consume large quantities of alcohol, you will probably find it extremely difficult to start drinking more moderately or become alcohol-free. Even though you may feel better when you don't drink alcohol, it will still be hard to resist when everyone around you is enjoying a drink.

I have seen an example of crab mentality when I have immigrated to England from a much poorer country in Eastern Europe. Initially, I lived in a working class area in a less than desirable city. But to me, even that city was much wealthier than the city in my home country I moved from.

I saw opportunities everywhere. Perhaps, it wasn't really obvious how to become truly wealthy, but it was extremely obvious to me what needed to be done to enter a cosy middle class lifestyle.

England had free vocational and academic education and the city I used to live in wasn't an exception. The demand for professional jobs for the people with the right qualifications was high. Those professions paid well, which was especially felt in a city that was cheap to live in. And some of those professions required only a couple of years of education.

But to my surprise, many people in the area I lived in didn't see any of these things. To many of them, the world outside their working class area didn't exist at all. And I have even met some people who have spent their entire lives never visiting any place outside of their city!

In their environment, everyone who aspired to do anything other than a factory or construction work was ridiculed by their peers. In the local school, everyone who studied well was bullied. And I've heard too many times how parents taught their kids that people from the "sharp-elbowed middle class" were bad.

If those in your environment you trust the most keep telling you something while you're still young and the capacity for critical thinking hasn't developed yet, the idea that they keep telling you will get deeply ingrained in your brain. And if that idea is that the people who are one step above you on the socio-economic ladder are bad, it will be extremely hard for you to ever move up the socio-economic ladder. You will have to get to that step of the ladder to move any further, but your subconscious will make it hard for you to put the right effort in to become the kind of person that you've been taught to hate.

Another feature of that community that I observed was that some parents in the community never wanted their kids to be more successful than themselves. That manifested in their urge to sabotage the efforts of their kids to achieve anything substantial, regardless of whether that urge was conscious or unconscious.

For example, even though secondary education was free, students still needed some means to support themselves. So, the biggest asset that any teenager could have while doing secondary education was supporting parents.

However, I've seen time and time again how some parents would insist that their teenage child would be required to pay their fair share of rent as soon as they go to college. Many of those parents genuinely believed that such action instilled good work ethic in their kids. But in reality, it often deprived those kids of their future.

To be able to pay rent, a teenager needed to find a job. But the only type of job they could get with the minimum level of education and no experience was an unskilled minimum wage job. Because of this stress that a teenager has never been taught how to deal with, he or she would prioritize immediate earnings over education. And because of that, the person would be severely limited in their career choices in the future. Yes, they would still progress to supervisory positions if they work hard. But they will be at a severe disadvantage compared to someone who has spent their youth studying hard professional skills.

But the important thing to note is that none of these things were done by anyone out of malice. People in that community genuinely believed that a rough working class life is the only type of life that was possible for them and, in their mind, they were doing the best they could to prepare the next generation for such a life.

This, perhaps, was an extreme example of how your surroundings can affect your life in a major way. But the fact that your surrounding has such a power over you is still applicable in any type of a community.

How does the above example of these complex social dynamics help us understand how our colleagues and peers, who we regularly spend time with, mold our mindset? Well, even though you may not live in a community similar to this, the crab bucket principle works everywhere, even in professional settings. Choosing a wrong work environment may put brakes on your career.

As a programmer, you may be entirely surrounded by programmers who insist on only ever doing bare minimum. Those people can spend their entire career not knowing any best practices and writing code that barely works.

In such an environment, you may even be ridiculed if you insist on doing things properly, just like those kids who studied well were ridiculed in that school in a blue collar area.

And how can you even develop good programming habits if nobody in your environment has any? Or how can you even believe that someone from your town can indeed become an exceptional programmer when everyone you know isn't one? Perhaps, it's only the rich kids from nice areas who make it big.

This is why it's critically important to filter what kind of people you want to interact with the most. And to the best effect, what you can do is create an echo-chamber that will keep reflecting the right ideas back to you.

What is an echo-chamber?

The term "echo-chamber" refers to a social environment where your thoughts and ideas are reflected back to you. Essentially, when you talk to people in this environment, there is hardly ever any disagreement. People who occupy that space tend to agree on many things.

Echo-chambers never consist of just random groups of people. They are formed when people with similar interests join together.

Eventually, due to how our brain wants us to fit in, such a group evolves into something where its members are very close to each other in their views. And that's how echo-chambers are formed.

Essentially, it's just like a big empty room with a lot of echo, as the things that you express are almost identical to the things you hear back from other people.

There are many examples of social groups that can be classed as echo-chambers. Perhaps, the most extreme example of an echo-chamber is a religious cult. This is where members are indoctrinated to have identical beliefs and any dissent is severely punished.

Political parties are another good example of an echo-chamber. And the more radical a political party is - the stronger the echo-chamber. So, a cult-like communist party would be a stronger echo-chamber than some moderate centrist party. [7]

But because the definition of an echo-chamber in a social context is a scale of sorts, pretty much any permanent social circle has the characteristics of an echo-echo chamber, unless it's a kind of a circle that encourages the discussion of opposing ideas, like a debating society of any university.

Humans are naturally inclined to form echo-chambers. After all we are social animals and feeling as a member of a tribe is a natural instinct that gives us a major evolutionary advantage. Our strong natural desire to belong is precisely why we tend to make friends with those who share our preferences, interests and the outlook on life, or even modify our behavior to fit in. [0]

But at the same time, echo-chambers are what makes us biased. If we keep hearing the same ideas over and over again, we will stop questioning them and will just accept them as the truth, even if it isn't objectively true.

As humans, we have many cognitive biases. And the stronger the echo-chamber is - the more reinforced these biases will become. That's precisely what makes us develop a distorted view of reality. For example, instead of trying to find out if some idea is objectively correct and looking up a whole range of quality sources, we just pay attention to the sources that support our belief, regardless of their quality.

And often, we do it purely to prove our opponent wrong rather than gain knowledge. After all, our own confirmation bias has already convinced us that this idea is true.

The problem with echo-chambers is that an idea repeated many times will form well-developed neural pathways in your brain. This is why it then becomes very hard to accept an alternative idea, even if all evidence says that it's actually correct.

And in the digital age, all of these negative features of an echo-chamber have been amplified by the web, especially by social media. The algorithms behind all the content-hosting platforms have been designed in such a way that we receive more and more content that's like the content that we've already interacted with. Over time, the only type of content you'll be seeing is the content you've already expressed preference for.

But the fact that echo-chambers inevitably skew your opinion in a particular way doesn't necessarily make all of them bad. And even being biased in some way is not necessarily a bad thing, even though this word usually has a bad connotation.

First of all, every one of us is biased. There is no getting away from it. Every one of us has some preferences.

Secondly, echo-chambers are effective conduits of ideas and self-belief. Despite all the negative connotation associated with the term, echo-chamber can be the best tool for building a growth mindset in the quickest way possible.

So, getting out of an echo-chamber, as many people like to suggest, can be counter-productive advice that you shouldn't necessarily follow. Not all echo-chambers are bad.

Why not all echo-chambers are bad

It's not an echo-chamber itself that is bad. It's the thoughts and ideas that are constantly shared inside of it that make it either good or bad.

Yes, a cult is an example of an echo-chamber. But so is a mastermind group that was put together by a bunch of ambitions and highly-successful people. However, the former is a type of an echo-chamber you should seek to avoid, while the latter is a kind you should strive to join.

Big tech companies are aware of these echo-chamber principles. Therefore they carefully select their candidates to ensure that only people with high standards make the grade. Likewise, they ensure that their employees are always surrounded by other people of high professional standards. For example, during onboarding of new hires, Google assigns a "buddy" to a newly hired person, who then actively helps the new team member to build a social network within the company. [9]

Another example of a good echo-chamber is a seminar organized by performance coaches. You may wonder, why people like Tony Robbins are so popular and why their seminars are in such a high demand, despite costing several hundred (or even thousand) dollars to attend?

Well, it's not because of the information provided in those seminars. You can get all the same information from a book that costs very little or a web podcast that is free. [10] But reading one self-help book once is not enough: the conceptual understanding of principles behind success is not enough to make you successful. You will need to practice these principles until they become second nature to you. But it's extremely hard to practice something if your environment is not optimal for it or if your social circle actively disapproves of these ideas.

The reason why people (who often are already successful by conventional standards) willingly pay such a large sum of money to be there is so they get surrounded by the right kind of people. And they get immersed in and motivated by the ideas that will potentially make them better.

When you are surrounded by like-minded people for a number of days in the row, your mind is a fertile ground for productive ideas and growth. Your environment will confirm the ideas' validity. And this will help your subconscious mind to accept them.

Seeking an echo-chamber consisting of people whose ideas also have a growth mindset and want to succeed is probably the best thing you can do.

For software developers in particular, a good example of a good echo-chamber is an intensive coding bootcamp. They can be so effective that, once you graduate from one after just a few months, you may be able to outcompete computer science graduates that have spent years earning their degrees.

There are different types of coding bootcamp, but intensive ones are the ones where students spend 70-80 hours per week for months on end. You can't participate in such a bootcamp and have a job at the same time, even if it's merely a part-time job. [11]

There will be coaches that will push you to your limit and there will be other students who you will regularly speak to. So, for months, you will be in an environment where pretty much all of your waking hours are spent surrounded purely by the ideas on how to learn to code in the quickest way possible. And being surrounded by ambitious people who don't mind putting long hours in will motivate you to be the best you can be.

Coding bootcamp is a perfect definition of an echo-chamber. With a schedule as intensive as this, you will simply not have time to socialize much with people outside of the bootcamp. And you will probably not have much cognitive capacity or desire left to consume irrelevant content either.

And it's not hard to find examples of successful alumni of coding bootcamps. Some go on to become software developers, while others go even further and start their own companies. For example, Alyssa Ravasio has started an online tent-booking service called Hipcamp after graduating from a coding bootcamp. [12]

But not everyone will have enough financial means of time to go through a coding bootcamp. Likewise, even if you've graduated from a reputable bootcamp, accidentally picking a bad echo-chamber can cause you to erode a good mindset that you have worked so hard to build.

So, if you know that echo-chambers can be good or bad, what signs should you look out for to distinguish between the two? Well, the general principles of it are fairly straight-forward.

Dodging the bad echo chambers

There is a simple rule of thumb that will help you to distinguish between good and bad echo-chambers. Of course, just like any other rule of thumb, it doesn't work in every single situation. But nonetheless, it works in most situations.

Good echo chambers are the ones that you deliberately seek out and pro-actively try to join.

Bad echo-chambers are the ones that you get dragged into without realizing.

The process of entering a bad echo-chamber is akin to placing a frog into a boiling pan.

So, if you throw a frog into boiling water, it will feel the pain instantly and will jump out. However, if you place it into a pan full of cold water and start boiling it, as a cold-blooded creature it will not notice the gradual change in the temperature and will just stay there until it boils to death.

The same happens to human beings who get dragged into a bad echo-chamber. For example, let's imagine a person who is largely apolitical. Perhaps, he or she feels strongly about a thing or two that's happening in the society. But other than that, they don't care about politics at all. There are many other things that they prefer to spend their time on.

But then, one day, they get engaged in conversation with someone about one of those few political things they care about. And this person convinces them to become an active supporter of a particular political movement, because the point of view that this person has is shared by this movement.

This person joins the movement. After all, it's nice to be surrounded by people who agree with you on issues you have a strong opinion about. And there don't seem to be any other things that this movement stands for that this person disagrees with, even if he or she doesn't particularly care about any of those. Some of them may even seem stupid, but who cares?

Initially, this person retains their personality, but fast-forward a few years and this is no longer the case. There is hardly anything left that used to make this person unique. Instead, they behave and sound just like another typical member of that particular political movement. All they talk about is what their party stands for. And they seem to not only agree with everything the party stands for, but even actively express support for those ideas they previously thought as stupid.

So, what exactly happened? Well, since the person joined the movement, they started to constantly interact with other supporters. And they gradually started absorbing the ideas that have been circulating in the movement.

Eventually, they stopped questioning such ideas. They have just started accepting them as their own. And they started spending more and more time on politics and less and less time on the things that used to interest them. Eventually, politics has become their obsession.

But still, even though political movements have the power to indoctrinate their members, they are still fairly benign, as far as echo-chambers go, unless the movement is truly radical and authoritarian. The worst types of destructive echo-chambers are cults, which can ruin lives.

The negative echo-chambers that you are likely to encounter as a programmer probably won't ruin your life, but they can still put your career on hold.

Toxic work cultures you may encounter as a developer

If you end up in a sub-standard software development team where people do the bare minimum and cutting corners is the norm, over time, you can become just like the rest of the team members. All your ambitions of having a spectacular programming career would disappear. It doesn't matter how ambitious and hardworking you are: in a bad echo-chamber this mindset of doing the bare-minimum might infect you too.

You'll be that frog that doesn't notice that it's being boiled. Initially, you might be determined to go the extra mile and be better than everyone else on your team. The fact that everyone on it is a slacker won't annoy you, and you'll still socialize with them in order to fit in.

But there's only one of you against several of them. Eventually, while being surrounded by mediocrity, you will start to accept it. Perhaps there will even be pressure to do so. For example, the management might tell you to ditch the unit tests, because this weird practice that they don't understand makes it much longer to write the code.

Even if you try your best to explain the reason why best practices need to be implemented, your team may not get on board with it. Things were working the way they are before you joined. So why change them? It's not Google, after all!

The main reason why it's a big problem in software development is that even mediocre companies with teams like this would pay a reasonably good salary to a software developer that would allow them to have a fairly comfortable life. And this is why it's so easy just to succumb to the temptations and forget your ambitions if you can have an easy 9 to 5 job.

If you have already ended up in a toxic workplace like this, you should try to leave it as soon as possible. Leaving such a place may not always be easy, especially if you are just at the start of your career and haven't built enough experience to try and move jobs yet. But shortly, we will discuss the tools that you'll be able to use to stay on top of your game even while you have to endure the toxic work culture. These tools will eventually make it easy for you to leave a toxic workplace and find a workplace that's helping you to develop the growth mindset.

But toxic echo-chambers you may end up in as a developer aren't limited just to your workplace.

Be aware of different mindsets in your friends and family

Also, try to spend as little time as possible with people who can potentially be jealous of your salary. As a software developer, you will probably be earning more than average, even if you work for a small software house. Therefore, if you come from a relatively poor background, chances are that you'll know a lot of people who earn significantly less than you.

Some of these will feel jealous and will try to sabotage your career progress, either consciously or subconsciously. Perhaps, they will constantly talk about how wealthy people are no good. Or maybe they'll ridicule your work ethic.

So, look out for a potential "crab bucket" situation. And if you ever realize that you are in one, try to get out of it as soon as possible.

Of course, sometimes people that pull you down are your close relatives or your childhood friends that you can't just cut off completely from your life. And it's not always jealousy or malice that will prompt them to say things to you that will discourage your ambitions. Sometimes they will say that while genuinely believing that they are giving you good advice.

In this case, just keep contact with them to a minimum. Keep in touch with them. Meet up with them on occasions. But keep them at an arm's length. Don't let them into the innermost personal circle.

How excessive comfort can lead you into a bad echo-chamber

One of the main reasons why bad echo-chambers are the ones you fall into rather than consciously choose to be in is that they are more comfortable to be in than good echo-chambers. To get into a good echo-chamber, you would often have to leave your comfort zone, while getting into a bad echo chamber just happens on its own if you stay in your comfort zone. This is why the best thing you can do to dodge a bad echo-chamber is learn how to not get too comfortable.

You should look out for getting complacent in your career. There are many ambitious developers who work really hard while they have just been employed. But after some time, while they are familiar with all the processes, they allow their enthusiasm and ambitions to fade away.

Over time, they become comfortable and allow the comfort to take over. They just start going with the flow, occasionally getting promoted. And when enough people within an organization do this, this is precisely how the above mentioned toxic work environments come into being.

Just be aware of how strong the lure of comfort is. If you want to be an elite-level developer, comfort is your enemy. As Steve Jobs once said, you should stay hungry. **[13]**

So, get into the habit of doing what's right rather than what's comfortable. Those things will become comfortable over time anyway, because this is how habits work, as you already know. You'll need to deliberately aim to join a good echo-chamber. And there are quite a few types of echo-chambers that will aid you in your programming career.

Using good echo-chambers to become the best programmer you can be

In general, if your goal is to have a great software development career, you should aim to spend as much time as possible in an environment populated by software developers who are already known for their greatness and those who have similar goals to what you do. And luckily, there are many specific ways to make it happen.

Join a bootcamps and/or university

If you are just getting started in your career or perhaps just thinking about becoming a software developer, then one of the best things you can do is to join a coding bootcamp or enroll at a good university.

Of course, neither of these options are suitable for everyone. Both require a considerable financial commitment, unless you live in a country where higher education is free. However, universities in such countries tend to be highly selective, so you usually would need a stellar academic history to get into a university.

But being good at getting good grades at school doesn't necessarily translate into being a good professional programmer. So, even if you don't qualify for a university, this doesn't mean that you cannot become an exceptional programmer. It simply means that academia is not your thing.

In the places where university courses are paid for by students, coding bootcamps tend to be a cheaper option. But it still requires a substantial time commitment. And intensive bootcamp is called intensive for a reason. It's way more intensive than a university course. Not everyone will be dedicated enough to spend up to 16 hours a day learning how to code for months on end.

Neither of these options are critical to you becoming a high-achieving professional software developer.

But if you can attend either a bootcamp or a university course related to programming (computer science, software engineering, etc.), then you probably should. It can help you develop the right mindset in the shortest time frame possible.

We have already covered what makes a coding bootcamp an echo-chamber. Spending all your waking hours surrounded by professional programming teachers and ambitious and hard-working students affects your mindset in a positive way. But so does a university.

People don't enroll in a university to learn some new skills. Virtually anything that university teaches can be accessed free of charge online. Or can be taught in much cheaper vocational training courses.

People go to university to get immersed in a particular kind of a social environment. And this characteristic is what makes university education so valuable.

In my case, I have, at one point, realized that I didn't need a university degree to get a good job. But I've only realized this after having been to a university. University environment was what changed my mindset.

A good university is a place where you are surrounded by highly ambitious students and teachers who are dedicated to their craft. It's the opposite of a crab bucket. Instead of everyone in your environment pulling you down, your peers will be pushing you up.

But regardless whether you have been to a university or not, it's better to maintain a useful echo-chamber or two throughout your career. And for a software engineering career, there is nothing better than regularly attending developer conferences.

A caution on bootcamps and universities

If you are just starting your journey and want to consider a coding bootcamp, make sure you pick a good one. Coding bootcamps are largely unregulated, so they can be of varied quality. And the worst thing that can happen to you in your career as a programmer is acquiring many bad habits or a wrong mindset that will take you a long time to change. In an extreme scenario, having a bad bootcamp coach may even make you think that programming is a wrong career for you, while in reality it could have been the most fulfilling career you could ever have had.

Absolutely anyone can open a business and call it a coding bootcamp. Therefore, while choosing a bootcamp, verify its reputation. If it's really new, then perhaps you shouldn't join it. Yes, it might be good. But it has equal chances of being bad. There is no way of knowing.

If it doesn't have many reviews or any reviews at all, perhaps you should skip it too. Another red flag is when it has many reviews, but all of them are either one-star or five-star. It's not very difficult to hire a bot farm that will generate many positive reviews for you. And when you see that almost all reviews for a particular product or service are either one-star or five-star, it's a really good sign that one has been purchased.

One-star reviews are probably genuine ones, while five-star reviews are fake ones to offset the organic negative rating. So, a bootcamp with such reviews is probably beyond bad.

I would choose a bootcamp that is well-known and well-regarded in the industry. If any well-known software development house endorses it, then it's probably a good bootcamp. After all, it's got its stamp of approval.

It's even better if a bootcamp is actually organized by a well-established educational institution, like a university or a college. This means that it will probably adhere to high standards, just like any certified educational institution would normally do.

The same applies if you are planning to join a university. Not all universities are made equal. And there are some bad ones. As a software developer, I have interviewed my fair share of absolutely awful computer science graduates that didn't even know the basics and didn't show much enthusiasm towards the profession.

So, just like with the bootcamp selection, research the university ranking. Try to find out what proportion of its graduates end up employed by reputable companies.

Attend conferences

All major software companies organize high-profile developer conferences. Microsoft does an annual Build event. Google does Google I/O. And so on.

There are plenty of developer conferences out there. Some are expensive, while others are cheap or even completely free. Some run for several days, while others run for just a couple of hours. Also, distinguished developers that are well-known in the industry are often invited to stand-alone talks of workshops.

Of course, these kinds of events get recorded and you can see most of its content on YouTube, which makes them even more accessible. But even though a recorded presentation will give you the same information as the original one, it won't provide the same echo-chamber effect that attending an actual conference would.

Conferences are where you surround yourself with like-minded people. And this is where you can actually interact with those superstar developers that everyone in the industry knows.

Perhaps the greatest benefit of these conferences is that, when you meet those celebrity developers, you realize that there is nothing special about them. They are just ordinary people who have developed the right habits and a growth mindset.

And this is what helps you to develop a growth mindset too. Seeing that it doesn't require a genius to become a great developer will motivate you. And if you interact with people like this repeatedly, your belief that you can become a great developer too will solidify. And that's how you acquire the right mindset to become the best you can be.

But developer conferences don't happen every day. Nevertheless, there is an even better way of maintaining an environment around you that is conducive to the development of the right mindset for building a spectacular programming career. You can try to join one of the big tech companies, like Facebook, Amazon, Apple, Netflix or Google, which are collectively referred to as FAANG.

Set your sights on the best tech companies

Of course, there are other big tech companies that are just as good as FAANG. Microsoft is one of them. And so is a consultancy firm ThoughWorks. If it's a major tech organization that you have heard about - it will probably be a really good place to work in. At least, from the perspective of developing your career.

It's not the fact that these companies pay more than smaller IT companies that is the main reason why you should probably consider working for them. And it's not that their names will look good on your résumé, which will make you a highly desirable employee within the industry. Of course, both of these things are true. But the greatest benefit comes from the fact that working for one of such companies will shape you as a great professional.

Big tech companies are ultimate echo-chambers. Each has its own corporate culture that every employee gets immersed in. And they all have extremely high standards in terms of selecting the candidates.

You don't have to be particularly smart to join one of these companies. But you certainly need to be ambitious and diligent. And when you are constantly surrounded by developers who hold themselves to high standards, it's inevitable that you will become such a developer too. Holding yourself to high standards will come natural to you. It's just a cultural norm in the environment that you spend most of your time in.

But getting yourself ready to join one of the big tech companies takes time. And it may take you many unsuccessful attempts. So, while you haven't joined one, you can join a few web forums of meetup groups dedicated to software craftsmanship.

Find a group that matches your interests

But remember that it's not just being a proverbial "fly on the wall" in those groups that helps you to develop the right mindset. You need to interact with other participants.

Building the mindset is just like developing a skill. You won't develop it merely by consuming information. You will develop it by practicing it. Mindset in particular gets built by being exposed to ideas and accepting them. And nothing will help you to accept the ideas quicker than expressing them yourself. This is precisely why you need to be an active participant in developer forums.

But just make sure you join good forums. There are plenty of bad ones out there. So always verify the reputation of any given forum before joining it.

Don't let your enthusiasm fade away. Stay an active participant in software development forums. Attend conferences. Keep yourself up to date with all the new technologies in your niche. Only this way you'll be one of those rare software developers that everyone wants to hire. Otherwise, you'll just be an obscure blob in a gray mass of mediocre programmers.

And the last important thing about the echo-chambers is that you should only enter the specific ones that are biased towards constructive ideas about career development. You probably don't want to become biased in the other areas of your life.

All echo-chambers make you biased, so choose only those that will make you biased in a beneficial way. If you become biased towards the idea that being a great software developer is possible for everyone who is willing to put sufficient work into it, it's a good type of bias to have. But if you develop other types of biases, for example, the ones that will give you a highly distorted view of reality or make you intolerant towards certain categories of people, you should leave such echo-chambers.

It's the latter type of bias that gives the negative connotation to the term "echo-chamber". It's the areas such as politics and science where you should seek diverse opinions and perhaps even follow authors that you don't necessarily agree with. But when it comes to your career development, stay in the echo-chambers that will aid it.

And with modern technology, one of the best tools to help you to get into echo-chambers is social media. Yes, we have already discussed how social media can be the biggest enemy of your professional development. But if you use it in the right way, the same algorithms that have been originally designed to steal your attention can be consciously applied by you to make your social media apps an echo-chamber that you want to be a part of.

There are various ways you can hijack social media algorithms to turn them from hindrances into useful tools for yourself. And this is precisely what we will be discussing in the next chapter.

References

1. Courtney E. Ackerman - Big Five Personality Traits: The OCEAN Model Explained - positivepsychology.com, 15 April 2021
2. Donna L Lively - How To Recognize and Overcome Victim Mentality: Learn why taking responsibility is the most

important step to you health and well-being and the steps to take to open the door to anything you desire

3. Jerrell Forman - Critical Thinking: What You Should Have Been Taught About Decision-Making, Problem Solving, Cognitive Biases, Logical Fallacies and Winning Arguments

4. Carl Hulse - Confirmation Bias: Inside Washington's War Over the Supreme Court, from Scalia's Death to Justice Kavanaugh - Harper

5. Davide Donelli - I Am Your Mirror: Mirror Neurons and Empathy - BlossomingBooks

6. Carliss D. Miller - Exploring the Crabs in the Barrel Syndrome in Organizations - Journal of Leadership & Organizational Studies, Vol 26, Issue 3, 2019

7. Remy Cross, David A. Snow - Radicalism within the Context of Social Movements: Processes and Types - The Journal of Strategic Security, Volume 4, winter 2011

8. Sarah Rose Cavanagh - Hivemind: The New Science of Tribalism in Our Divided World - Grand Central Publishing

9. Ben Mulholland - Why Google's Onboarding Process Works 25% Better Than Everyone Else's - process.st, 3 August, 2018

10. Tony Robbins - Awaken the Giant Within - Simon & Schuster Ltd

11. CODING BOOTCAMPS IN 2021 - YOUR COMPLETE GUIDE TO THE WORLD OF BOOTCAMPS - https://www.coursereport.com/coding-bootcamp-ultimate-guide

12. Lauren Stewart - These 10 Founders All Started at Coding Bootcamps - Course Report, 25 October 2016

13. Steve Jobs - How to live before you die - TED Conference, Stanford University, June 2005

CHAPTER 5

SUBDUING THE ENEMY: USING SOCIAL MEDIA TO YOUR ADVANTAGE

Think about what people are doing on Facebook today. They're keeping up with their friends and family, but they're also building an image and identity for themselves, which in a sense is their brand. They're connecting with the audience that they want to connect to. It's almost a disadvantage if you're not on it now.

--Mark Zuckerberg

You already know how social media was deliberately designed to monopolize your attention. This turns social media into a significant obstacle on your path of becoming a successful software developer. Those algorithms that have been developed to obtain as much of your attention as possible can prevent you from developing productive habits and can make it extremely hard to do deep work, both of which are absolutely essential for success in the tech industry.

However, the same algorithms can also be used to your advantage. After all, despite being well-designed, those algorithms are still relatively dumb. They are dumb enough to be manipulated with the right types of behavior.

With the right behavioral tweaks, you can trick your social media apps to only show you the content that is useful to your career goals and/or will help you develop yourself as a better person. Those tweaks are not necessarily intuitive, but once applied, they can actually turn social media into something that will accelerate, rather than hinder, your career.

So, how exactly can this happen? Well, there are two types of benefits that social media can give you if you use it in the right way:

- **Better inputs**: Social media is extremely effective at creating echo-chambers and gets regularly criticized for this. [1] But you now know that echo-chambers are not always bad. Echo-chambers of the right kind are actually one of the most effective tools for building the growth mindset that will align with your goals.

- **Better exposure**: As well as helping you to immerse yourself in the right type of information, social media can also help you to build your personal brand. It can help you to get noticed by potential recruiters, employers or clients. It's much easier to gain such exposure with the help of social media compared to building it all offline.

But before you can start actively taking advantage of social media, you need to make sure you have built the habit of using it in a disciplined manner. Otherwise, it will become a significant obstacle on the path towards your goals instead of being a tool that will accelerate you towards them.

To recap, you will need to get into the habit of doing the following things:

- Delete unnecessary apps.

- Turn off external notifications.

- Fine-tune the in-app notifications of your social media apps.

- Don't automatically follow recommended content.

- Have a plan for what you need to do and for how long.

- Use browser tools to reduce recommended content.

- Recognize and avoid obvious clickbait.

- Limit screen time.

- Don't use social media during specific times each day.

Make sure you are comfortable with these points. Some of them may take some time to get used to. But neglecting them may allow social media algorithms to slowly drag you back into the habit of getting distracted by social media, which is a stronger disadvantage to your career development than any potential advantage gained from any of the techniques we are about to discuss.

Before you can start consciously using social media, you need to make sure you aren't being used by it.

But if you have mastered the habit of disciplined social media use, you are ready to start manipulating its algorithms to your own advantage.

How social media algorithms can actually help you

The key point about social media algorithms is that they are not as smart as many people think. Yes, they are complex and truly sophisticated. But they are also highly predictable. And it's this predictability that makes them susceptible to being manipulated.

Let's recap three techniques that I have personally found to be effective against the negative aspects of social media:

1. Unfollow anyone who regularly posts content that triggers a strong disagreement in you.

2. Have at least one day per week of a complete social media detox.

3. Deliberately seek useful content that will aid you with achieving your goals.

And it's actually the last point that provides an overview of how social media algorithms can be manipulated.

Indeed, when I say "manipulated" while referring to social media algorithms, I am not talking about any complex and counterintuitive hacks, akin to the ones that cybercriminals apply. No, most of these manipulations are simple changes to your user behavior that, over time, will completely change what you see on your social media feed. Instead of being a major source of distraction, social media will become a treasure trove of useful information.

Let's recap that the algorithms closely pay attention to what kind of content you interact with. They want to determine what kind of content is the most interesting to you so that you spend more time on the platform. You will keep seeing more and more of the type of content you've already engaged with. The algorithms are designed this way because their creators want you to spend as much time on their platforms as possible. And seeing more of the content you are interested in is what will keep you on the platform for longer.

So, in a nutshell, to fill your social media feed with content that is actually useful to you instead of being distracting, you will need to actively engage with a lot of content of this type, while ignoring everything else.

But it's not necessarily a quick process. It takes time for the algorithms to recognize the patterns in your content-consumption habits and determine that specific types of content may no longer be relevant.

Keep in mind though, it probably won't clear your timeline of distracting content completely. If you've been online for long enough, you may have noticed that the recommendation engines would occasionally offer you some content that's completely unrelated to what you've been looking at recently, but is similar to the content you've been regularly consuming in the past.

Or sometimes you will see the content randomly popping up that is in no way related to any type of the content you consumed. There are various reasons for this. Perhaps, you just happen to share some characteristics with a group that is statistically likely to be interested in such content. Or maybe the platform is conducting an experiment on you without any of your knowledge. [2]

So, your Facebook timeline will not become a treasure trove of useful information overnight. And it will never become completely devoid of distracting content. But still, your social media platform will become a useful tool for your career development rather than its hindrance. The amount of helpful content on it will far outweigh the content of the distracting kind.

As an aspiring elite programmer, you will want your timeline to be composed of links to technical articles, software development podcasts, posts from the thought leaders of the industry and, perhaps, other types of useful content about personal and professional growth that isn't specific to programming. And it's within your power to fill up your timeline with these types of content.

But there is a very important caveat. Before you can utilize the techniques of algorithm manipulation, you need to be fully confident that you don't have any traces of social media addiction.

Why you need to prioritize digital minimalism over intentional algorithm manipulation

Deliberately manipulating social media algorithms may be harder than it sounds, especially during the early stages. The content that is actually useful for your professional development tends to be complex and clever. But by default, you will still be surrounded by a lot of dumb, but highly entertaining, content. And this content is much more compelling to our brain than the clever and engaging variety. [3]

There is nothing wrong with watching mindless entertaining content now and again. All of us need a break from hard cognitive work now and again. But fun content is addictive. And this is precisely why we should try our best to minimize it

If you've been a regular social media user for years, you would probably have been largely using it on autopilot. If so, then your feed will probably be mostly filled with the dumb but entertaining posts. And this is precisely why you need to develop the habit of conscious and disciplined social media usage before you can start deliberately manipulating the content delivery algorithms.

Without this discipline, you can fall right back into the habit of using social media unconsciously. After all, that's what years of using it have probably conditioned your brain to do. And if you do fall back into the habit of compulsive usage of social media, then it will, once again, become your biggest source of distraction that will prevent you from developing yourself as an outstanding professional.

So, before you can use social media in the way that benefits you, you need to make sure that you are comfortable with not using it for some time at all. And this social media fast should not feel like a chore. To verify that you don't have anything that resembles social media addiction, you should be able to abstain from social media while not constantly thinking about using it again.

We already discussed why willpower is a limited resource. Using too much of it on unimportant activities prevents you from utilizing it on important ones. But because programming consists of hard tasks that often require willpower, it's especially important for a programmer not to waste it.

This is why, for a programmer who has, over the years, developed a habit of frequent social media usage, it may not be a good idea to completely abstain from it for several days. It would be much better to gradually develop the habit of highly disciplined social media use.

How to be a digital minimalist

First, you should try to minimize social media usage in the ways we have already discussed. Once you have applied all the necessary configurations to your account to minimize unwanted interruptions and you got into the habit of using social media consciously rather than compulsively, then you can try to abstain from it.

If you can go for a few days without opening your timeline and this is relatively easy for you, only then you should start fine-tuning your timeline by making the user behavior adjustments that will manipulate the algorithms.

To make sure that you don't slip back into the compulsive social media usage, there are, essentially, two habits that you need to develop. All of the action points we have discussed before (see chapter 1) (except the ones that involved changing app configuration) aim at developing these two habits.

- **Using social media only during specific time windows:** If you can do this, then your brain has been trained not to make you compulsively pick up your smartphone several times throughout the day. You have full control over when you go to social media platforms.

- **Controlling your reactions to the content you see:** If you can avoid interacting with clickbait when you see it and avoid entering a pointless discussion with someone who has posted something that you deeply disagree with, then you have full control over your timeline. And so you are ready to fine-tune it.

Of course, you will probably not be able to do either of those 100% of the time. After all, you probably remember how social media was deliberately designed to be addictive and distracting. But even if you can do these two actions most of the time, then you are ready to start fine-tuning your timeline.

Remember that you may get dragged back into autopilot mode at any time. And you should be ready to leave the app as soon as you start to feel like you are wasting time on it again. Also, you should be prepared to stop using social media for a few days in a row when necessary.

Don't forget that notification bell, infinite scroll and "like" button are still highly addictive features, even if your timeline is filled exclusively by good quality content. Even with this kind of content, you may still fall into a mental mode of zombie-like autopilot and spend hours upon hours in your app. That's why having a degree of control over your social media usage is so important.

But social media is not only about content that the algorithms deliver to you. After all, those platforms were originally made for social interactions between people.

An important thing to note is that the combination of social interactions and personalized content-delivery algorithms makes social media perfect for creating echo-chambers. After all, the term is most frequently used precisely in the context of social media. And, as you know that echo-chambers can be both good and bad, that's good news. The same algorithms you can manipulate to deliver the right type of content to you can also help you to automate the creation of echo-chambers of the right kind.

Automate formation of a good echo-chamber

Social interactions form a major part of social media, hence its name. But those are not the only parts of social media.

Facebook can no longer be referred to as just a "social network", as it shows a lot of content to its users that has little to do with social interactions. You will see a lot of content appearing on your timeline that none of your contacts on the platforms have shared.

And that's what makes the methods that we have discussed so far so effective at fine-tuning your timeline. It's those recommendation engines that will deliver you the content similar to what you've been regularly interacting with.

But there are still social elements to it. You will still regularly see what your contacts have been posting. And you will regularly see posts from the groups you are a member of.

The algorithms that push stuff onto your timeline don't just try to interpret the content of the posts you regularly interact with. They also look at what people and groups you like to interact with. And so you will be seeing more posts from them.

Interacting with only carefully selected types of content will do a good job of turning your social media platform into a treasure trove of useful information. But to maximize its potential, you will need to take care of its social aspects too.

So, here are some concrete steps you can take to filter the content on your timeline that comes from your groups and direct contacts:

1. **Unfollow everyone who regularly posts distracting content.** We have previously talked about unfollowing anyone who regularly posts content you strongly disagree with. But this is going one step further.

To recap, unfollowing is different from removing the contact. The former merely prevents new posts from this person from being displayed on your timeline, while the latter is completely removing the connection.

It could be someone you still want to be a friend with in real life. After all, it's well known that people often act differently on social media from the way they do in real life. [4]

The reason why you should unfollow those who regularly post things you disagree with is so you don't get dragged into long and pointless discussions. But you may also have someone in your contacts who regularly posts something that doesn't trigger much of an emotional response, but is still distracting.

It could be some funny memes. Or it could be some quotes that don't make sense outside their original context. Those posts are benign, but they will still catch your attention, potentially breaking your state of focus.

So, it's better to unfollow such people. If they post something that you do occasionally find entertaining, you can still go to their profiles and check their latest post while you aren't working. But to leverage your social media as a career-building tool, this kind of content should not be automatically displayed on your timeline.

2. **Do occasional audits of your contacts.** Sometimes, removing people from your contact list is precisely the right thing to do. Maybe you have added someone there without much thought. Maybe you don't even know them in person. In any case, if you aren't getting any value from having any particular contact in your list, you should consider removing them.

   Besides contributing towards the removal of irrelevant content, removing certain people from your contact list comes with other benefits. For example, you may not want to share all your social media activity with everyone, but if you add someone you barely know into your contact list, they will see your "friends only" types of posts.

When someone you don't know has access to your personal information that you intended to only share with friends, they can then use it to try to perform a phishing attack on you. Or they may share publicly your post that you wanted only your friends to see. Therefore, letting anyone join your network is generally not a good practice.

3. **Deliberately seek inspiring people to follow.** Many celebrities are on social media, and this includes well-known developers, like David Fowler and Scott Hanselman. Those are people that publish a lot of useful and insightful content.

   Of course, unless you are also famous, very few of such people would agree to add you as a friend on their Facebook page. But pretty much all social media platforms allow you to follow people without actually making a connection with them.

   This way, any public posts they publish may appear on your timeline

4. **Do occasional audits of groups you are a member of.** Social media allows you to join various interest groups. And there are plenty of those that are specifically intended to make you a better software developer. At least, that's what they claim to be. And many of them are indeed helpful.

   There are plenty of bad groups on social media too. Some are just dedicated to time-wasting activities. Some are full of people that post things that would trigger a strong emotional response in you. Some have barely any activity at all.

   So, it pays to occasionally sit down, go through each group that you are a member of and ask yourself: "What value do I get from being a member of this particular group?".

   If the answer is "definitely none" or you can't get a coherent answer, then it's probably time for you to leave this group.

   And this also applies to groups that are dedicated to software engineering or various aspects of personal and professional development. Not all the groups are what they claim to be.

Yes, a group may have been created with the best of intentions. But since then, something went wrong.

Maybe it doesn't have a good team of moderators, so it's full of spam. Or maybe it's full of advertisements and was actually intended to be this way. Or maybe it's actually a good group, but it's primarily inhabited by programming novices, while you are an experienced developer already.

Whatever it is, if any particular group doesn't serve you, just leave it. This will guarantee that you will never see irrelevant posts from it on your timeline.

5. **Seek to join groups that are full of people that you would want to emulate.** Social media platforms have plenty of groups that will help you grow as a professional. Those are the ones that are frequented by the kind of people that you want to emulate.

   These groups will be exactly the echo-chambers you are looking for. The content in them will be of the right kind and quality. And you will be able to participate in useful discussions.

   If you come from a "crab bucket" environment that we have discussed before and you don't know enough people to form a productive echo-chamber with, these groups are the best tool you can use to meet people outside your normal social circle. Even if your daily situation doesn't allow you to meet those you aspire to, these online groups will allow you to network with people that you wouldn't have met otherwise.

   But remember that, as we have discussed before, not all groups on social media do what the title says. And you can't always preview the content inside a group. Many groups are private and you can't see anything until one of the admins approves your request to join. This is another reason why you would need to occasionally perform the audit of the groups you are a member of.

And that's it. Implementing this small bunch of fairly simple steps will turn your social media platform into an echo-chamber of the right kind. Once you perform these actions, you will rarely see any distracting and otherwise unhelpful content on your timeline again. Instead, you will always be presented with engaging and insightful posts.

But this is not where fine-tuning the content delivery algorithms of social media stops. You can go one step further and fine-tune your internal notifications.

Get notified about the stuff that really matters

On social media platforms, there are two types of notifications - external and internal. External notifications are the ones that make your smartphone vibrate when something noteworthy has happened on your social media profile. Internal notifications are the ones that make a number appear on your notification bell when you actually open your social media app or visit its website in your browser.

External notifications on social media are the ones you should completely switch off. As someone who aspires to become the best software engineer you can be, you don't want to get distracted while you are doing some deep work only because someone "liked" one of your posts. But internal notifications are a different story.

Of course, just like we've discussed before, you should still be extremely selective when it comes to internal notifications. That notification bell has been deliberately designed to draw your attention. This is why the numbers on it are usually brightly colored. And you don't want your attention to be hijacked by telling you that one of your friends, who you barely know, has "liked" some post that you aren't even remotely interested in.

Well, the good news is that performing some of the steps that we have already discussed, like clearing your contact list, unfollowing certain people and removing yourself from useless groups will substantially reduce the amount of irrelevant notifications you would get. You will no longer get notified if someone you barely know just had a live stream. Or that someone you don't know has posted something in a group you are a member of.

And, like we covered in **chapter 1**, by fine-tuning the overall notification settings on your profile and on individual groups, you will reduce irrelevant internal notifications to almost none.

This is easy on any modern social media platform. Because the companies that run these platforms get constantly scrutinized for manipulating user behavior, they have made it incredibly easy and intuitive to adjust your notification settings. **[5]**

But sometimes you can reap some dividends from selectively enabling some of the notifications that you would normally keep disabled. For example, there may be some exceptionally useful group that consistently produces high-quality content. Or maybe some group is known for occasionally organizing useful offline events with a limited number of places. So, if you missed the post, it may be too late.

Those are the groups where you perhaps want to enable all notifications. In this case, getting notified about something that's not 100% relevant but is still somewhat useful is better than missing an important and time-sensitive announcement.

But how to decide whether any particular group is worthy to enable all notifications on? Well, I would use the following criteria:

- **A group is known for organizing events that are useful for your professional development.** In the context of software development, those could be hackathons. Those could be conferences that involve well-known IT companies. Or those could be talks organized by celebrity programmers.

  You already know how much positively these events contribute towards the development of a growth mindset. So you don't want to miss those announcements.

- **A group has members who are well known and highly regarded in the industry.** If such a person joins a group, it's probably because he or she enjoys sharing their experience and insights. And such a person would have a lot of useful things to say.

You don't want to miss posts from them. So you would probably want to enable all notifications in such a group.

The only exception is when such people join groups purely for fun and don't post anything there other than funny memes. In this case, you should probably stay in such a group. After all, these kinds of people are highly protective of their time and rarely join forums of sub-par quality. But, in this case, you wouldn't want to be notified of every random post from such a group.

- **A group is known to regularly host constructive professional discussions.** It's like an industry-specific debating society. This is where you can actively share information, get your ideas tested and otherwise have great conversations with top-level developers that you aspire to emulate. Or maybe you can just be a proverbial "fly on the wall" and observe how highly experienced professionals discuss professional topics.

  Having all notifications enabled on such a group would ensure that you never miss an interesting discussion topic.

And the last point brings us to another great benefit that social media can offer you if you use it carefully. In **chapter 3**, we covered why soft skills are just important in your programming career as hard technical skills. Just as like it is with any other skills, you need to practice soft skills to become good at them. You need to build the right neural pathways to gain the ability to say the right things at the right times. And social media is one of the best tools to practice those in the safest possible environment.

Practice soft skills in a safe environment

There are several ways being part of high-quality tech groups on social media can aid you in development of your soft skills. After all, many of these skills are conversation-related and those groups are globally distributed conversation hubs.

These are some of the techniques you can use:

- **Observe the conversations and learn proper terminology.**
  Software development career is full of technical jargon. So, to be successful in the industry, you need to learn it.

  You will not learn all the terminology that professional programmers use from online tutorials and documentation. Just like any other profession, software engineering has developed its own jargon that has nothing to do with the official technical terminology.

  But learning the official terminology won't hurt either. You don't know what you don't know, so, as a beginner, you may not even have any idea where to look to learn the terminology. But if you take part in regular conversations with experienced professional developers, or even if you merely observe these conversations, you will learn most of this terminology naturally.

  And, of course, it's important to know the jargon. This will make you look like an experienced industry veteran. And it will make you more attractive to potential employers.

  The more conversations between top-notch developers are happening in a given group–the better.

- **Find people in the group to collaborate with.**
  Communication skills are just a subset of soft skills. But there are also others, such as time management and teamwork. And it's these soft skills that you can practice by collaborating with other people.

  Professional social media groups are full of programmers who participate in open-source projects or even in private commercial projects. So, it won't be hard to find somebody in these groups to collaborate with.

  And participating in such projects will give you more career dividends than just developing good teamwork skills. It will augment your technical skills. And it will add to the portfolio of the projects you've done, that you can later show to a potential employer.

- **Practice presenting your ideas.** A software development job is not exclusively about coding. You will be taking part in various planning meetings where you will be expected to share your ideas. And the more senior position you hold–the more frequent these meetings will be.

  Therefore, you need to master the skill of presenting your ideas to the public. And nothing is better for this purpose than a social media group.

  It's not a real project, where your boss may look unfavorably at you if you lack the skill of coherent communication. If you haven't yet developed the ability to communicate clearly, it doesn't matter. In the worst case scenario, your posts or comments will just not receive many responses. But in the best case scenario, someone may actually engage you in conversation and will point out the flows in your arguments. And it's these encounters that will help you to gradually build good communication skills for the future.

  And just observing how others present their ideas and mimicking them will also help you to improve your communication skills.

- **Practice debating with disagreeable people.** In a software development job, you won't always be surrounded by friendly and agreeable people. Sometimes, you will have to argue your case with those who aren't on-board with you, whether it's your boss, people from other departments or your own team.

  And you may also recall that your salary as a programmer doesn't only depend on your technical skills and years of experience. The ability to negotiate also plays a big part in it.

  But when you negotiate your pay, you inevitably face someone who wants to keep it as low as possible. For you, it's an income, but for your employer or your client, it's an expense. Therefore you need to be able to present your case coherently and deal with objections.

Even if you don't win negotiations, you still need to be able to accept the defeat with grace. However, most people aren't naturally good at accepting "no" as an answer, as this is interpreted by our brains as social rejection. [6] Likewise, most people aren't naturally good at contradicting someone's opinion, as humans naturally fear conflicts for the physical and psychological damage it may cause. [7]

But being able to deal with a loss of an argument and not being afraid to initiate an argument are the skills that can tremendously improve your career. So, to overcome your natural tendencies, you need a safe environment to practice them in.

And, once again, nothing can be safer than a social media group on the internet. It's much easier to actively disagree with someone online than in real life. After all, even if our conscious mind realizes that we are talking to real people, to our subconscious those are just pixels on the screen. [8]

But by the same token, the responses you will get online may be nastier than in real life. And at the beginning, those might be hard to deal with. But eventually, it's precisely these responses that will help you to grow enough of a thick skin to be able to deal with verbal conflicts in your real career.

And if an argument on social media goes too far, the consequences for you are unlikely to be as severe as they would have been in real life. The other person might just block you. Or, if the other person goes too far, you can always just block them. You can't block your co-workers or clients in the same way.

But, of course, you still need to be careful what you say. If you say something that's generally considered inappropriate, it may result in negative consequences for you in real life. If the content of your posts can be considered excessively offensive, someone might even inform your employer or your clients. [9]

Remember that the point of this exercise is to gain the ability to practice debate with those who disagree with you, so you can re-use these skills in a professional environment. Therefore don't just initiate random arguments for the sake of an argument. Only participate in those arguments where you genuinely believe your opponent to be wrong. And try to start the discussion by asking meaningful questions, rather than simply attacking the other person's point of view. Maybe, you will find that it's actually you who was wrong. This way, all participants will gain value from the conversation.

And limit those only to professional subjects. Even though for many, their profession is their passion, work-related topics don't generate as much emotional response as, for example, politics and religion. Therefore, there is a greater chance for a debate not to disintegrate into a mess if you keep it within the context of programming.

And, by all means, stay polite and respectful. This way, not only will you enjoy the conversation, but it will also get you into the habit of arguing in a polite and respectful manner in general. And this will maximize your chances of winning such arguments in the future.

If you regularly engage in productive discussions on social media that serve both yourself and the people you interact with, the algorithms will notice. And those types of discussions you can join in will be another type of useful content that will occupy your timeline space.

The more diverse the useful content you regularly interact with, the less space there will be on your timeline for distracting or otherwise useless content. And that's how your timeline will become an ultimate echo-chamber that will serve you.

So far, we had a detailed discussion on how to turn a social media app into a useful echo-chamber that can help you to develop the right type of mindset for your career development. But there is also another obvious feature of social media that you can utilize–its ability to showcase yourself to potential employers and clients.

How social media can help you to build your personal brand

As well as being a tool to help you develop a growth mindset and allow you to practice soft skills, social media is also a tool that allows you to define how the world sees you. And this is something that can make or break your career in tech. You might be the most skillful programmer with excellent communication and teamwork skills. But if your public social media profiles look bad, nobody would want to hire you.

The content you put on the web contributes to the development of your personal brand, whether you like it or not. You might not be into sales and marketing, but every time you try to negotiate with a potential employer or a client, you are selling something. More precisely, you are selling your skills. So, if you don't make it as easy as possible to showcase your skills, you will be outcompeted by those who do.

Brands have been invented for a reason. An organization that owns the brand will do everything it can to build the best possible reputation for it. If they succeed, the general public will immediately think of something they can trust when the brand name is mentioned.

It works the other way too. If an organization neglects to build the reputation for its brand, it will either fall into obscurity and will get outcompeted by others in its niche, or it will inadvertently build a bad reputation for itself. In the latter case, mentioning the name of the brand to someone will generate a negative response. And such an organization will not survive very long.

But brands are not exclusive to organizations. As a highly skilled professional, you need to worry about your personal brand. If your name isn't known, you will lose out in the job market to those who are known, even if they are much less skillful than you. Likewise, if you haven't been careful with your public online image, reputable companies may not want to hire you.

Of course, there are many ways you can build your presence online. But social media with its algorithms is one of the best tools to help you develop your personal brand.

How to build your online brand

Here are some relatively simple actions you can take to get started:

- **Do regular audits of your public profile.** Not everything you post on social media will be seen by the public. Most platforms allow you to make the content visible only to your contacts or make it completely private, so only you can see it.

  But if the content is inappropriate, there is nothing that stops one of your contacts from taking a screenshot, even if they can't share it. And it's inappropriate content that can completely kill your professional reputation. If it has been shared, it will stay on the internet forever. Once the genie is out of the bottle, you can't put it back in. You can't remove the content that has already been screenshotted and shared, even if you removed the original post.

  For public content, it's even worse, because it could be absolutely anyone who can screenshot the content they have deemed inappropriate. But even if nobody screenshots any of your content, it's still there for everyone to see it. And if a potential employer decides to Google your name, you will not be shortlisted for a position in their company.

  And even if you no longer post anything that anyone could find inappropriate, you may still get in trouble for your old posts from the times when you were less thoughtful and mature. Plenty of people, including some celebrities, were fired from their positions because of something they posted years ago. **[10]**

  This is why you should occasionally sit down and do an audit of your public profiles on social media. Go through your posts and, for each one, think about whether or not enough people will find it offensive or inappropriate. If so, either delete it or make it private.

  Not everyone has the same sense of humor. Something that one person finds funny another person would find highly offensive.

And you wouldn't want to risk your professional reputation over something that made you laugh for a minute and then you've forgotten about. After all, you can still share any type of jokes and stories with your personal circle of friends.

> Remember that freedom of speech doesn't give you freedom from consequences.

- **Avoid posting about sensitive subjects, such as politics and religion.** These two subjects trigger a strong emotional response in people. And if you actively express your point of view on either of those, you are guaranteed to attract strong agreement from some and strong disagreement from others. And you don't want to be on a blacklist of some potential employers over something that has absolutely nothing to do with your professional skills only because one of their directors happens to disagree with your political views or religious preferences.

  You will not do anything useful anyway if you just share your views on politics or religion on social media. All you'll do is help to perpetuate the negative aspects of social media that we have discussed in chapter 1. Nothing kick-starts long emotional arguments better than an emotionally-charged subject. And social media companies absolutely love it when their users participate in long discussions and sacrifice a lot of their attention to their platforms.

  If you want to talk about either of those subjects, it's better to do it offline with people who would appreciate such a conversation. If you really want to do it on social media, only ever do it in private groups that have been specifically dedicated to these types of conversations.

  If you want to express your political opinion, there is no more effective way of doing so than a ballot box.

  On emotional subjects like these, you won't change people's opinion anyway. Those who agree with you will just express agreement, while those who disagree with you will engage you in an argument. And it's precisely these types of emotionally charged arguments where the risk of accidentally writing something inappropriate is the greatest.

- **Regularly post insightful content and make it public.** You don't have to create original content. Not everyone is good at it. And you certainly don't have to be a master writer.

  The easiest way of filling your public profile with insightful content is by sharing what others have created. Any post, article or video that provides some helpful information is suitable, especially if they are related to your professional field. After all, the authors have created it to be shared.

  But don't just share it as is. Add some of your own words. Perhaps, write a short description of what the author is saying. Or write your opinion about the content, saying what you liked or disliked about it.

  Use appropriate hashtags in your posts. This will help the algorithms to make your post searchable with the right keywords. This may get engagements from other people who are interested in the subject and will help you to get known in the online world.

  If you do this for a while, then any potential employer or client who would want to find out who you are will see that you are actively consuming helpful types of information. And you aren't just sharing some random links without providing any evidence of actually reading the content. They'll see that you are sharing your own thoughts on professional subjects.

  If you have your own blog–even better. But if you'll regularly post your thoughts about professional subjects on your public social media profiles, you will give an impression that you are really interested in those subjects and you know what you are talking about.

- **Put a description of yourself that you want the public to see.** Every commercial brand has a story that people behind it want the public to associate with the brand. So, if the platform allows you to put a description of yourself on your profile, that will be the equivalent of such a story in relation to your personal brand.

In this description, you should use keywords that you want to be found under. For example, you may put the names of programming languages or other technologies that you are an expert in. You may also put years of professional experience in the field or a brief description of some successful projects that you've completed.

This is important for two reasons. Not only will it be the first thing the potential employers or clients will see while searching for your name, but search engine crawlers may actually make it easier for your profile to be found when people specifically look for those keywords that you've put there.

Search engine optimization (SEO) relies heavily on keywords. [11] So, if you use the appropriate ones, various algorithms of the web may bring you some job offers from unexpected places.

- **Add links to any external sources that will look good in the professional world.** If you have a GitHub page with the code samples that you've authored, it will help potential employers to see the quality of your work. If the work is of fairly good quality, such a link will look good on your profile.

If you have your personal website, YouTube channel, or if you teach on Udemy or Skillshare, those links will also look good on your profile, as long as the content you've created on these platforms is of a reasonable quality.

The quality of such content doesn't have to be perfect. Even if you aren't 100% happy with its quality, putting links to it will still help you. Any reasonable person will understand that nobody is born with perfect skills.

Perhaps the quality of the code you've written or other types of content you've authored is not quite there yet purely because you don't yet have much experience. But if there is evidence of continuous improvement, then it's not a problem.

If your content is of good quality, you will give yourself an advantage on the market by making it easy to find. But even if it's not the best, the links to it on your profile will still show to the potential employers that you are kind of a person who is truly dedicated to your craft. You will still have an advantage on the market over those who don't maintain GitHub repositories, don't blog and don't publish training courses.

The only times you should not post a link to your projects on your public profile is when you truly think that the quality of your work is bad or if the content of those repositories is confidential. That's when the extra work you've done can actually compromise your professional reputation rather than improve it.

These steps will make it easier for you to find professional opportunities. Not only will you present yourself in a good light to those who have actively searched for your name, but your profile may be found by someone who is looking for a subject matter expert in a particular technology niche. Also, as only relatively few people customize their public profiles this way, you will stand out.

Applying various techniques to make social media algorithms work to your advantage is good, but an important thing to remember is that not all social media platforms are made the same. There are those where you can apply all of the techniques we've discussed so far, while there are also others that are completely useless to you outside the context of entertainment.

Not all social media apps are made the same

All social media platforms differ from each other. And not all of them will be useful to your professional career. That doesn't mean that they are completely useless. You can still occasionally use them for entertainment. But performing the above-mentioned algorithm optimizations on them would be completely fruitless, as they won't give you any advantage in the world of software development.

TikTok, Instagram and Snapchat are some of the best-known examples of those. They were never designed for anything other than entertainment. So use them sparingly if you want to use them at all.

Which social media apps can benefit you

But there are also the ones that will help you to supercharge your career. And perhaps the most important of those are the following:

- **LinkedIn (https://www.linkedin.com).** For a professional programmer, this is the first social media platform in the order of importance. After all, it was specifically designed for career development. And it has very little irrelevant or distracting content.

  Every technique we've discussed will work well on this platform.

- **Quora (https://www.quora.com/).** This is a social network that's specifically dedicated to people posting questions and long-form answers to them. And then the system of nested comments under each answer allows you to have discussions with people.

  This is a perfect platform for filtering out irrelevant content. The questions are split into topics and you have a fine-grained control over which topics you follow. And there are also discussion groups.

  The answers to the questions on this platform are indexed by Google, so if you are able to give a good answer to a topic, it may appear on the first page of search results when somebody is researching this topic.

  Every technique we've discussed will work on Quora, including profile customization to make it stand out.

- **Facebook (https://www.facebook.com/).** Facebook is a universal social media platform that started out as a way for friends to stay in touch. It has since evolved into a hub with loads of different types of functionality.

138

Almost every technique we've discussed will work on this platform, except, perhaps, certain profile customizations.

But this is a platform where you should be careful. It has huge quantities of all sorts of content, most of which is just time-wasting and distracting. And it comes with perhaps the strongest behavior-modifying algorithms built into it. So you need a reasonable amount of discipline to be able to manipulate it. Otherwise it will manipulate you.

- **Twitter (https://twitter.com/)**. Twitter is a microblogging website that limits the number of characters you can put in each post. So, it's good for sharing links or brief insight, but not good for sharing long-form content.

  Because of the strict character limit, it's not the best platform to engage in discussions on. But it's a good platform for building a personal brand by filling your public profile with insightful posts.

  But the timeline on the platform can still be fine-tuned to display only the content of the right kind, giving you the desired echo-chamber effect.

- **Reddit (https://www.reddit.com/)**. Reddit is a platform that is heavily used by programmers. It's specifically known for the anonymity it gives to the users. And because of the anonymity, it's not the best platform to build your personal brand on. But it can still be useful for your professional development.

  It consists of many different subject areas, so-called subreddits. And this makes it fairly easy to filter out irrelevant content. Some of them are dedicated to helpful content that you want to see more of.

  Because Reddit is frequented by tech professionals, it's fairly easy to find good subreddits on it that you can follow. To an extent, it's a platform that facilitates discussions between users.

Be warned though. The anonymity that the platform provides sometimes makes those discussions go sour. If you make a mistake about a subject, the replies you may get will be far from being polite and respectful. So it's a good platform for sharing insights, but not the best for debating content.

So far, we had a look at how you can adjust your environment to facilitate the development of the growth mindset that will help you to supercharge your career as a software developer. We first covered the adjustments you can make in your social circle. Then we moved on to manipulating social media algorithms, so those platforms would continuously give you the right types of cues.

All of these actions are external. But there is also some internal work you can do to help you to evolve into the best possible version of yourself as a person and as a professional. In the next chapter, we will be talking about actively developing your attitude to everything that happens within your sphere of influence.

We will be talking about the concept of extreme ownership, which was first coined by US Navy SEALS, but can be used in any field by anyone who aspires to be a high-achiever. This certainly includes those who aspire to become elite-level software developers.

References

1. Matteo Cinelli, Gianmarco De Francisci Morales, Alessandro Galeazzi, Walter Quattrociocchi - The echo chamber effect on social media - PNAS, March 2, 2021
2. Kashmir Hill - Facebook Manipulated 689,003 Users' Emotions For Science - Forbes, Jun 28, 2014
3. Peter G Stromberg Ph.D. - Why is Entertainment so Entertaining? - Psychology Today, August 29, 2009
4. Gaia Vince - Evolution explains why we act differently online - BBC Future, 3rd April 2018
5. Eric Ravenscraft - Facebook's Notifications Are Out of Control. Here's How to Tame Them. - New York Times, May 30, 2019
6. Kirsten Weir - The pain of social rejection - American Psychological Association, 2012, Vol 43, No. 4

7. F. Diane Barth, L.C.S.W. - Why Is It Hard to Say "No" and How Can You Get Better at It? - Psychology Today, January 15, 2016
8. Amber Dance - Communication: Antisocial media - Nature, 09 March 2017
9. Americans and 'Cancel Culture': Where Some See Calls for Accountability, Others See Censorship, Punishment - Pew Research Center, May 19, 2021
10. Bryan Bishop - Writer-director James Gunn fired from Guardians of the Galaxy Vol. 3 over offensive tweets - The Verge, Jul 20, 2018
11. Brian Dean - The Definitive Guide To SEO In 2021 - Backlinco

CHAPTER 6

EXTREME OWNERSHIP – WHAT PROGRAMMERS CAN LEARN FROM US NAVY SEALS

Extreme Ownership. Leaders must own everything in their world. There is no one else to blame.

--Jocko Willink

In the previous two chapters, we had a look at how to build a social environment that will help you grow as a professional programmer. First, we covered the importance of deliberately surrounding yourself with echo-chambers of the right kind. Then, we had a look at how technology can be used to automate this process.

This covers the most important components of your external environment that you can change to aid you in your growth. Now, we will go through the things you can change on the inside your core beliefs.

Your core beliefs don't get developed in a vacuum. Being constantly surrounded by the right kind of people will have an effect on yours. To some extent, you will adopt the beliefs of the people you regularly interact with. But the most powerful core beliefs that you can have are the ones that you have deliberately worked on developing yourself.

The idea of extreme ownership is one of such things that you have to deliberately work on and that, over time, will completely change who you are and how you view life. It's an idea that will help you to fix all of your problems, evaluate your past mistakes, gain trust among your peers and superiors and, within realistic limitations, help you to achieve anything you want to achieve in your life.

Extreme ownership is the idea that you accept responsibility for everything that is happening in your environment. It's the idea that even if something that has happened was genuinely outside of your control, it was probably still your prior series of choices that led to this outcome. Likewise, even if you had no control over an event, according to the concept of extreme ownership, you still control your reaction to the event.

It's a conceptually simple idea. But simple doesn't necessarily mean easy. Depending on your mindset, it may take some time to fully embrace this idea. If you are someone who has a habit of thinking that your successes or failures are mostly caused by external factors outside your control, it may be hard for you to start embodying the attitude of extreme ownership. It will take you more time and effort to start living by this set of principles than it will someone who is in the habit of taking personal responsibility for their successes and failures.

But the good news is that living your life by a certain ideal is nothing but a habit. Even if it initially feels hard to embrace a particular ideal, it gets easier with practice. And, over time, it just becomes a core belief that you live by. It becomes a part of who you are.

Even if you are someone with an external locus of control, you will still be able to eventually start living your life based on the principles of extreme ownership. It just may take you longer. But if you persist at practicing these principles, you will, eventually, get there. [1]

Extreme ownership may seem like an excessively heavy burden to carry, but it's definitely not. It will only seem heavy to those who misunderstood what it stands for. Therefore, before we have a look at what extreme ownership is, let's see what it isn't.

- **Extreme ownership is not about solving everyone else's problems.** If somebody's problem affects you directly or indirectly, you need to respond to this. But solving the problem for somebody else is not necessarily the right response.

It's up to you to assess the situation, make the decision and then own the consequences of that decision. But, depending on the situation, the right decision might be to make them personally accountable. Or to guide them on how to solve the problem. Or even to just completely remove yourself from the situation.

- **Extreme ownership is not about accepting the blame for what other people did.** Again, if someone needs to be accountable for their actions, they should be accountable. But it's up to you to assess if there was anything that you could have done to prevent this mishap, if there is anything you can do now to control the damage and if there is anything you should do differently in the future to prevent such mishaps from happening.

- **Extreme ownership is not about victim-blaming.** It's not a religious idea that you are an evangelist of. Therefore you must not expect everyone around you to practice it.

  Injustice is real. Bad things do happen to people due to no fault of their own. And it's not up to you to blame them. It's up to you to deal with the outcomes, if those affect you in any way.

- **Extreme ownership is not about putting up with injustice.** It's the opposite. It's about doing everything you can to stop the injustice.

  And it's not necessarily about fighting the form of oppression that you are affected by. If your goal is merely to stop yourself from being oppressed, removing yourself from the situation might be the right decision. It's primarily about making decisions and owning their outcomes.

  For example, extreme ownership doesn't compel you to change the culture in a toxic company. But it does compel you to make sure that you don't work for a toxic company or a team.

Now, since we got out of the way, let's have a look at what the idea of extreme ownership is and where it came from. Then, we will look at specific examples of why extreme ownership is almost guaranteed to enhance your software development career if you choose to embrace it. After that, you will learn what to do if embracing this idea is particularly hard for you.

Where the idea of extreme ownership came from

The term "extreme ownership" was coined by Jocko Willink, a retired US Navy SEAL officer, who then became a famous author, podcaster and a businessman. Although the term itself is fairly new, the philosophy that this term represents has been practiced for thousands of years. It's very similar to what famous stoic philosophers taught. [2]

Jocko Willink, along with his ex-team mate from US Navy SEALs, has co-authored a book entirely dedicated to the concept of extreme ownership. [3] And since releasing the book, he has spoken at length about the concept in his podcasts, interviews and public talks.

There is one particular personal story that he has shared multiple times that provides perhaps the best example of extreme ownership being applied. It was something that happened in Ramadi in Iraq while he was stationed there with his platoon during an anti-insurgency operation. Here is a brief recap of this story.

There was a friendly fire incident where US soldiers got into a firefight with friendly Iraqi army soldiers, mistaking them for the insurgents. As a result, one Iraqi soldier was killed, while two were wounded and one member of the US Navy SEALs was also wounded.

The high command was angry with the outcome and was looking to fire someone over the incident. As the commanding officer of the platoon that was engaged in the incident, Jocko Willink had to describe what went wrong and tell the higher-ups who was responsible.

Jocko gathered his platoon in front of the investigating officers and started asking every soldier who they thought was responsible for the incident. And every one of these soldiers said that it was them who was responsible, as it was a specific action that the soldier did that contributed towards what happened.

But after hearing what the soldiers had to say, Jocko said that they all were wrong. It wasn't any of them that was responsible. As the commanding officer, he was responsible for the actions of the entire platoon.

Perhaps, it wasn't him personally that has misidentified the friendly Iraqi forces as the insurgents. Perhaps, it wasn't his personal actions that made things go not according to plan. But it was him that had to approve all the plans and factor in any contingencies. And he said that, as the commanding officer, he failed to do it properly.

He has admitted that such a thing was hard to do. His personal ego took a big hit. But he gained a lot in return. Both his superiors and people under his command started trusting him more. And nobody got fired as a result. Instead of assigning blame, steps have been taken to ensure that such a thing doesn't happen again.

What are the principles behind the idea of extreme ownership

So, what makes this kind of accepting ownership "extreme"? Well, in this case, Jocko Willink wasn't even expected to accept full responsibility. He was within his right to find specific people who made the mistake during the operation and assign all the blame to them. Those people would have been punished and the incident would have been resolved.

But the outcome of this would be the loss of trust among the people under his command. After all, everyone makes mistakes. But if you happen to be in an environment where you are severely punished for unintentional mistakes, it's unlikely to be an environment where you are encouraged to be fully honest and transparent with your superiors.

But extreme ownership doesn't imply that you always have to assign blame to yourself when bad things happen. Yes, you do admit your mistakes if you genuinely feel that they are yours. But the key characteristic of extreme ownership is that you accept personal responsibility for any situation that you have any influence on.

Accepting responsibility is not the same as accepting the blame. In the former case, you accept that you will do everything in your power to resolve the situation while being honest and transparent with those who watch you doing it. In the latter case, you just give up and accept the punishment.

Jocko Willink didn't just accept personal responsibility to put his humility on display. He did it because he followed the principles of extreme ownership, which are as follows:

- **Do everything you can to create the best possible outcome out of a situation that you have at least some control over.** In his case, the best possible outcome was that such a situation never happens again. You cannot undo what has already happened and nobody will win if some people just get punished.

- **Be fully honest and transparent while taking the actions.** Jocko could have resolved the situation in many different ways. For example, he could have deceived the commanding officers to prevent people from his platoon getting punished. But deception could have cost him dearly in the future.

  When you practice extreme ownership, you don't merely resolve the situations that you can resolve. You actually do it in an honest and transparent manner. This way, you are actually showing people that you own it. And even though there is a risk, the benefits of being honest far outweigh the risks.

Now, you can see that extreme ownership is not merely some kind of a quasi-religion or a randomly conceived philosophical teaching. Even though it's very similar to what some philosophers and spiritual leaders have been teaching, the idea of extreme ownership is fully pragmatic and is based in reality.

But you might be asking, how relevant is extreme ownership to the world of programming? After all, it's worlds apart from what people in the military do!

Well, this principle is applicable in all types of a career and in other areas of life beyond the career. And it's especially relevant when people are striving to become elite.

What can elite programmers learn from elite soldiers

Even though the office environment in a tech firm can't be any more different from an active war zone and, as a programmer, you are unlikely to be dealing with life-or-death situations, many things that programmers deal with are kind of similar to the things soldiers deal with.

Of course, you will not have anything similar to a friendly fire incident, or any type of a situation where somebody dies or gets wounded. But you will deal with your fair share of mishaps.

For example, you, or somebody else, may accidentally deploy a bug onto a production server, which will cost your employer a large sum of money. Your company's server may go down. Or your software may become a successful target of a cyber attack.

And, just like in the military, you will have elite team members and everyone else. It's exactly the same thing that determines whether you become the elite or not, beyond the specific skills that are needed for doing your job well–your attitude. Specifically, your willingness to take personal responsibility, learn from your mistakes and do what's right.

And even though, as a programmer, you will never have to deal with the aftermath of a friendly fire incident like the one Jocko Willink had to deal with, you will have to, occasionally, deal with serious incidents nonetheless.

The aftermath of a friendly fire incident is not much different from an aftermath of a catastrophic software failure. In both of these types of incidents, you will often see people pointing fingers at each other. But finger-pointing never resolves the situation. Therefore, the best way of dealing with IT incidents would be exactly the same as dealing with military failures–taking ownership.

When dealing with IT incidents, it doesn't matter who has caused these incidents. It matters that the incidents are resolved. And this is where extreme ownership comes into play.

The best way to gain trust in any career

When Jocko Willink took responsibility for the friendly fire incident, he not only resolved the situation in the best way possible, but also gained trust among both his superiors and the people under his command. And so will happen to anyone else who will apply the principles of extreme ownership in any career.

When some unforeseen circumstances happen, people won't always put themselves forward if they aren't directly responsible for the incident. They will just allow somebody else to be nominated to resolve it.

And there is nothing wrong with that. If you choose to only ever be responsible for those things that were directly assigned to you, you are still doing your job. But unless you start stepping up, it's unlikely that you will ever get promoted from your position.

Even though you do a specific job, you are still part of a bigger business. And the overall performance of the business affects you. If the business doesn't do well, it's you who won't receive the bonus or the pay rise. Or, if business performance is truly abysmal, you may even lose your job altogether.

Those who aspire to be leaders understand these things. And even though they still do their regular duties, they will step up wherever they can to resolve bigger problems that affect the business overall.

Or sometimes the problem that the business is having actually is of your own making. In this case, fixing this problem would be the right thing to do. But it will also matter what you will say when the problem becomes apparent.

Many people will protect their egos in such a situation. And even though they will admit their responsibility to a degree, they will come up with excuses to dampen the degree of their personal responsibility.

They will point a finger at various circumstances outside of their control that have led to this.

Maybe those excuses are honest. Maybe circumstances beyond their control have truly happened. But this is not the extreme ownership way.

The extreme ownership way is to swallow your pride and admit your failings. But instead of doing it in a submissive manner and apologizing profusely, offer the ways to fix the problem in the best way possible.

What are your thoughts when you hear someone making excuses or making an excessive amount of apologies? Even if all those excuses are actually truthful, the person making those excuses or apologies doesn't sound trustworthy. The person sounds even less trustworthy if they completely deny to accept any personal responsibility when responsibility is theirs.

You can see many noteworthy examples of this behavior in politics. You may recall many instances of a politician making some promises that he or she then fails to deliver on, while denying any personal responsibility for it afterwards. This is why politics is often considered to be one of the least trustworthy professions.

But who are the most trustworthy people you've met? Those would be the ones who accept personal responsibility without making any excuses. Those who show that they don't only act in their personal interests, but in the interests of the bigger organization would also be seen as trustworthy, especially when they do it consistently. Therefore, there is no better way of gaining trust in your career than practicing extreme ownership.

For example, the queen of the United Kingdom, Elizabeth the 2nd, is generally considered to be trustworthy. She has maintained a consistent public image. And, despite many public scandals happening inside the British Royal Family, she has never been personally tainted by any of them.

The same could be said about Mahatma Gandhi, who was the leader of the movement that liberated India from colonial rule. He practiced what he preached. And that's precisely why many locals have willingly followed him and colonial administrators respected him. [4]

And it applies to a career in programming as much as it does to any other professional career. There is no better way of getting noticed other than taking extreme ownership.

How a heightened sense of ownership makes you an effective programmer

As a programmer who has just developed a new feature or fixed some bug, it will be your responsibility to ensure that this change not only works, but doesn't break anything else in the system. And you need to make sure that the code you've written adheres to best practices, so it's easily readable and maintainable.

This is where programmers can apply extreme ownership at the most fundamental level. Instead of making excuses for how they were too time-pressed to write new unit tests or refactor the code to get it to follow SOLID principles and design patterns, they need to do due diligence. And the item shouldn't be marked as done until all these extra steps are completed. These are the actions that every good programmer is expected to do anyway, regardless of whether or not they know what extreme ownership is.

But programming is not only about writing code. It's about providing value to the business that has hired you. Those programmers who live by the principles of extreme ownership will understand that. And they will take responsibility not only for the specific code base that they work on, but also for a smooth operation of the business. At least, for those parts of it that they can actually influence.

The website is down while you are trying to develop a new feature? Yes, the development of the said feature might be your direct job, but the website outage is a much higher priority overall. After all, nobody needs the new feature if there is no website to put it on.

Will the company directors care if the new feature is developed on time? Maybe, but they will care more about the website outage being fixed as soon as possible. The feature can wait, while the outage prevents the business from operating. And if you accept personal responsibility for ensuring that business can operate again ASAP, they will notice that.

Or maybe you are in a team that develops new software features, while a separate team is responsible for software releases to production. Imagine a situation where some problem pops up that prevents the other team from releasing a new software version on time.

Once again, you can just tell yourself that it's not your problem and carry on developing new features. But if you look at the bigger picture, you'll realize that any new feature only becomes meaningful when it's actually released. And the quicker the problem with the current release is fixed–the quicker can you release the feature you are currently working on.

Or maybe that's a release of a critical bug fix that will put the company out of business if not applied on time. If this happens, then nobody will ever need that new shiny feature that you are working on.

But it doesn't only apply to incidents that the business has to react to. Extreme ownership is also exercised when you are being proactive to prevent incidents from happening and to prevent bad features from being added to the apps.

You can just carry on working on software development tickets that get assigned to you. And that's fine. Most software developers do this. But you can also influence which tickets make it into the list in the first place and which ones get pushed on top of the list.

If you take responsibility for the overall direction of software development processes, you may, one day, get promoted to a position where being responsible for the overall direction of software development processes is your actual job description. This is the quickest way you can become a technical lead or an architect.

Taking extreme ownership at your workplace is equivalent to adopting the position of a leader. Just like any other habit, it becomes better with practice. And if you become good at adopting a leadership position, any rational manager would be more than happy to give you the actual leadership position.

Extreme ownership is what makes a true leader. And this perfectly applies to senior technical positions, like a technical architect. Yegor Bugayenko, a famous technical architect and an author, said the following:

> *"Any software project must have a technical leader, who is responsible for all technical decisions made by the team and has enough authority to make them. Responsibility and authority are two mandatory components that must be present in order to make it possible to call such a person an architect."* [5]

But regardless of how good you are at accepting a technical leadership position, sometimes you will find obstacles on the way in the form of non-technical project stakeholders. Quite often, these people don't have a very good grasp on how software works. Unfortunately, those often are the people who actually make the key project decisions.

But the good news is that you can apply the principles of extreme ownership while dealing with these people. And by doing so, you can build a fruitful and fulfilling relationship with them, while making sure that the projects don't get overwhelmed by unreasonable requirements.

Use extreme ownership to deal with non-technical project stakeholders

Dealing with non-technical stakeholders is a pet peeve of many programmers. There are countless web forums and Reddit threads where programmers complain about how stupid their bosses or clients are.

When it comes to the bosses, the frequent complaints are that they don't care about programming best practices and see them as fads that only slow down the release process. You will also frequently hear about non-technical managers who use wrong performance metrics (e.g. the frequency of releases rather than the resiliency of the software) and promote wrong types of people.

At first glance, none of these things seem like they are under your control. After all, you can't get inside people's heads and make them think differently. You may just think yourself unlucky that you happened to get such a boss. But if you step back and think about the situation from the perspective of extreme ownership, there is actually a lot you can do.

First of all, you need to remember that those non-technical managers are not stupid, like some developers on those forums like to imply. You can't get into a top managerial position at a technical company if you are stupid. Every one of these people had to gain a lot of real business experience or complete some advanced education to get there.

Even though those people are non-technical, they are smart enough to understand the importance of programming best practices. And the most likely reason why they don't appreciate their importance is because nobody has managed to communicate it to them properly.

After all, they don't know what they don't know. So, unless you explain to them why you need to apply due diligence and implement best programming practices, those will be seen purely as things that prolong the release process.

So, if your managers don't understand the importance of the said best practices, it's your job to communicate it to them. If they aren't happy with you writing so many tests, explain to them that a little extra time required to write those tests is a small price to pay compared to a business-critical failure of the software that occurred in production due to some untested part of the system. If they are not happy about you spending time refactoring the code, explain to them that this little amount of time spent on it now will prevent the code from becoming unreadable and unmanageable, which would have resulted in any new feature taking unnecessarily long time to implement.

If you think that something is important but you see that the other party doesn't grasp its importance, the concept of extreme ownership obliges you to communicate it to them in the best way possible. And if you are dealing with reasonable people, they will appreciate it. They will see you as someone who is always ready to provide valuable feedback when the time is right.

The same applies to the managers who use wrong performance metrics. They probably do it because they don't know any better. So make them aware of why it's wrong and show them which metrics would actually matter.

Use extreme ownership to help you get promoted

One of the complaints that you will frequently hear about non-technical managers is that they promote wrong people. Many programmers get resentful when they see people getting promoted for their ability to talk smoothly rather than their technical skills.

But this is not necessarily a bad thing. The more you progress in your career, the more important communication skills become. Technical skills are the most important aspect of your career right at the beginning. But as you start to progress into leadership roles, soft skills become more and more important. [6]

So, instead of being resentful about the fact that you get overlooked for promotions while those with inferior technical skills get promoted regularly, why don't you accept that it's something under your control?

You have already identified that it's those who have great communication skills that get promoted. So, why not accept extreme ownership and build your communication skills to the same level as theirs?

If you are kind of an employee who already shows ownership for the entire project rather than a narrow set of specific tasks and you have shown yourself to be a great communicator, any sane manager would see you as a great fit for a leadership role, if such a role becomes available. But if you see that people in your organization are genuinely promoted for wrong reasons, for example, due to cronyism, then you can leave such an organization with a clear conscience. After all, nobody owns your career. You do.

But the usual pet peeves of software developers don't only include non-technical managers and office politics. I have lost count of how many times I've heard experienced programmers complaining about stupid mistakes made by junior developers. But it's also a situation that can be dealt with by taking extreme ownership.

Use extreme ownership to deal with incompetent newbies

Somebody asked the following question on Quora:

> *"What do novice programmers do that professional programmers find cringe-y?" [7]*

The question has been answered over 80 times. The answers included the following examples, among many others:

- Not using source control

- Commiting directly into the main branch

- Not writing unit tests

These things are annoying and they cost a lot of time and effort for senior developers to correct. But if you look at them from the perspective of extreme ownership, you will see that all of them are actually your responsibility. Every single one of them.

Let's start with the fact that junior developers don't know what they don't know. Yes, they may know the syntax of a particular programming language. But they don't necessarily know how to work in a commercial enterprise. And, as an experienced developer, it's your job to teach them. Otherwise, they will never know. And you will be condemned to forever continue fixing things after them while complaining about it on online forums.

Junior developers don't know how to use source control? Teach them. And make sure that they understand why they need to use it.

They are checking their changes directly into the main branch? Implement the systems that will prevent them from doing so. Put the tools in place that will allow programmers to only merge into the main branch the code that has been reviewed by senior engineers.

They aren't writing any unit tests? Maybe it's because they don't even know what unit tests are. So teach them. And make sure they understand the importance of these tests.

And exactly the same approach can be applied to absolutely any other thing that novice programmers do that they shouldn't. There is only one caveat though. If they continue doing those things despite being repeatedly taught otherwise, then it's actually time to make them accountable.

Accepting personal responsibility for other people's actions doesn't imply that you take away all accountability from them. On the contrary, it's about making sure that the expectations are outlined clearly, sufficient resources are provided and people are held accountable for their performance. As Jocko Willink said:

> *"When setting expectations, no matter what has been said or written, if substandard performance is accepted and no one is held accountable—if there are no consequences—that poor performance becomes the new standard." [3]*

So, if a disciplinary action is appropriate, it's your responsibility to administer it. And if all else fails and it's appropriate to remove a developer from your team, you should do it.

But extreme ownership doesn't only apply to the things inside your job. The practice should also be applied to the process of finding a job. And it's especially useful while dealing with pushy recruiters.

Use extreme ownership to deal with pushy recruiters

Recruiters, or head-hunters, as they are called in some places, are great. Because such a profession exists, you, as a professional software developer, no longer have to submit many manual job applications. If you have sufficient experience in the industry, all you'll have to do is make your resume or CV searchable. And then recruiters will do the rest. The ones who are aware of vacancies that they think you are a good fit for will start calling you.

But recruiters are commissioned salespeople. And just like any other industry that involves commissioned sales, the recruitment industry attracts its fair share of bad apples. Some of them are just excessively pushy, while others are outright dishonest. As a result, many developers end up accepting jobs that are inferior to the ones they were actually looking for. Or they waste a lot of time going through multiple stages of the selection process only to find out that the job is not suitable for them.

But if you take full ownership over the direction of your career, it becomes a lot easier to not get inconvenienced by bad recruiters. You shouldn't forget that the interview process is designed as much for you to evaluate a prospective employer as it is for the employer to evaluate a prospective candidate. And, as every employer would have a list of minimal standards that the candidate must meet, so should you have a list of standards for your employer.

The easiest way to filter out unsuitable job offers is to have a list of requirements that you will not be willing to compromise on under any circumstances. For example, you may want to have a rule that you will not accept commute time over and above a certain threshold. Likewise, you may choose to reject any offer that doesn't offer a salary above a specific amount. Or you may have a more complex set of rules, where you could be willing to increase commute distance by a certain amount, but only if the employer would offer a higher salary.

These preferences can be anything that resonates with you. Perhaps you aren't too bothered about the salary or commute distance, but it's crucial for you that the company allows you to have a good work-life balance. Or maybe you wouldn't want to work for a company that places their developers on-call to deal with tech support issues in the software that has already been deployed.

Whatever your preferences are, it's your responsibility to make a list of them. If your job requirements are set in stone, it will be easy for you to instantly reject any job propositions that don't meet those requirements. Your time won't then be wasted.

Yes, for some people, it might be difficult to say no to a recruiter, especially when they are exceptionally polite. However, as someone who takes full ownership of one's career direction, you should remember that they are primarily concerned about their own commissions and not your best interests.

Don't worry about making recruiters feel bad when what they offer doesn't meet your requirements. They are professional salespeople and dealing with rejections is part and parcel of their job.

And remember that, as salespeople, recruiters have been trained to be persuasive. So ignore all of their niceties and always think about your own best interests while dealing with them.

We have only covered some situations where the concept of extreme ownership in a programmer's career can be extremely useful. But the same principles apply to other situations too. For example, if you are a junior developer, it's up to you to gain the respect of your senior colleagues. Likewise, if the company you work for has an excessive red tape that everyone complains about, you might actually be able to do something about it.

Extreme ownership is a powerful tool. But for some, it may seem like something that's almost impossible to practice. But, as I stated before, the principles of extreme ownership work just like any other habit. You become better at it the more you practice it. And the best way to practice extreme ownership is to try to apply it literally everywhere.

Why accepting personal responsibility should be your default mode

You might not be a person who is used to accepting the responsibility when something has happened that's genuinely outside your control. If so, it will probably be difficult for you to take extreme ownership in a situation where your career is on the line.

But the good news is that there are plenty of much smaller and less pressing situations in your life where you can practice extreme ownership until you are comfortable with it. Those situations will feel safe, as the worst-case scenarios of making a wrong call would not be too bad.

You can start with small things. For example, when you are late because of the traffic, try not to apologize or make excuses, but simply acknowledge that you are late. And even if the traffic jam was genuinely caused by something outside of your control, try to acknowledge to yourself that unexpected things sometimes happen and you should have a contingency plan. So, in a way, it was still you that's responsible for being late.

There are other things you could try. For example, if you know that one of your friends is moving, be proactive and offer your help. From the perspective of extreme ownership, your friendships are part of your life. So it's you who are responsible for strengthening them when such an opportunity presents itself.

There are many other little things that you can practice extreme ownership on. And then, once you are comfortable with the practice and have started adopting the worldview behind it, you can start applying it in your career or business.

But, after reading about the application and practice of the concept of extreme ownership, you may wonder if it's not something that may put you in danger of being taken advantage of? And won't viewing everything in your life as your personal responsibility leave you burned out? Well, the answer to both of these questions is "no" if you apply the principle of extreme ownership correctly.

How to not get burned out with the burden of personal responsibility

One caveat about stepping out and being proactive in a workplace is that it only works to your advantage if you are surrounded by reasonable and conscientious people. But, unfortunately, not all work environments are like that.

You may end up working for a toxic boss or you may end up working in a toxic team, even if the organization itself is reasonable. And if you are in such an environment, being proactive will be seen as a weakness. People will take advantage of this. People will be creating situations where more and more work comes your way.

But extreme ownership is not about shouldering the responsibility of others. It's about owning your life circumstances. So, it's actually the opposite of allowing yourself to become a doormat.

It's about solving the problems that you are faced with in the best way possible. So, when delegating a particular task to other people seems to be the most appropriate action, this is what should be done under the framework of extreme ownership. But if you do choose to delegate a task, you still own it. So, it will still be up to you to make sure that the task is done.

Likewise, saying "no" when it's appropriate to do so is also part of extreme ownership. You don't only own your work. You also own your life and your personal boundaries. So, when you are dealing with a toxic work culture or unreasonable demands from your bosses or clients, it's your duty to enforce those boundaries.

The airline advice of putting your mask on first before helping somebody else put on theirs may seem callous, but when you understand the reason why, you see it is a form of ownership: You cannot help place a mask on someone else unless you are still conscious in order to do it. And this is applicable to the concept of extreme ownership: You prioritize your own mental health and wellbeing over the work-related projects that you do. After all, you won't be fully productive and useful to others unless your fundamental needs are fully met.

Extreme ownership is about owning your life as a whole. And this includes judging how much responsibility you can actually carry. If you see that increased burden of responsibility negatively affects other important aspects of your life, like mental health, by all means, reduce the burden. This will still be in accordance with the principles of extreme ownership.

And if you see that, despite your best efforts, the environment that you have ended up in is not the best fit for you, you should be absolutely unashamed and unapologetic about moving somewhere else. This is especially true if you've already done what you could to change things there. Your conscience will be perfectly clear if you leave such an environment.

Extreme ownership is like a muscle. It grows better with practice. So, if you aren't used to shouldering a lot of responsibility, you don't have to try to take responsibility for the entire project. Do it in small steps. Every time you practice extreme ownership, do so in such a way that you leave your comfort zone just a little bit. And, over time, you will become a different person—a highly capable individual that is respected and trusted by your peers and your superiors.

So far in this part of the book we have covered several ways that would help you to build the right kind of attitude to become an elite programmer that everyone would want to hire. First, we have covered the importance of surrounding yourself with the right kind of people and creating echo chambers around them. Then, we had a look at how technology can be used to automate the creation of such echo chambers. Finally, we had a look at how you can personally work on your attitude to develop a sense of extreme ownership, which equates to seeing things from the perspective of a competent leader.

Now, we will see how you can design your daily routines to help you with both building the right habits and the right mindset. We will borrow the principles that have been used by monks of various religions and denominations for millenia. It may sound surprising, but those can be very useful in the world of programming.

But it won't be as dull as it may sound. We won't be covering any religious practices or ascetic rituals. We will only take what will work for us and ignore the rest.

You will see that a properly designed routine consisting of these practices is far from being dull. On the contrary, it will help you to make your life quite exciting, while reducing time wasting activities to the bare minimum.

References

1. Nichola Tyler, Roxanne Heffernan and Clare-Ann Fortune - Reorienting Locus of Control in Individuals Who Have Offended Through Strengths-Based Interventions: Personal Agency and the Good Lives Model - Frontiers in Psychology, 15 September 2020
2. Seneca - Letters from a stoic
3. Jocko Willink and Leif Babin - Extreme Ownership: How U.S. Navy SEALs Lead and Win

4. M.K Gandhi - An Autobiography: The Story of My Experiments with Truth
5. Yegor Bugayenko - Code Ahead: Volume 1
6. Susan A. Dean, Julia I. East - Soft Skills Needed for the 21st-Century Workforce - International Journal of Applied Management and Technology, 2019, Volume 18, Issue 1
7. Quora - What do novice programmers do that professional programmers find cringe-y? - https://www.quora.com/What-do-novice-programmers-do-that-professional-programmers-find-cringe-y

CHAPTER 7

HOW MONK MENTALITY CAN MAKE YOU A SUCCESSFUL PROGRAMMER

Raise your quality standards as high as you can live with, avoid wasting your time on routine problems, and always try to work as closely as possible at the boundary of your abilities. Do this, because it is the only way of discovering how that boundary should be moved forward.

--Edsger Wybe Dijkstra

You may think of monk lifestyle as something as far removed from the world of programming as something can possibly be. After all, when people hear the word "monk", they probably imagine some religious devotee dressed in funny clothes who lives in some remote place far away from modern civilization. Such people seem to live an extremely dull life and avoid any worldly pleasures.

But as a programmer, you are the opposite. Instead of avoiding modern civilization, you actively participate in building it. And I bet you don't say no to exciting things. After all, one of the reasons why people choose to be software developers is to get paid well, so they can afford the lifestyle they want

But what if I told you that having a monk-like mentality is not about following a boring lifestyle and rejecting everything modern? And it's not about being a religious devotee either. You can take advantage of monk mentality even if you are a militant atheist.

Yes, monk movements have religious origins. They primarily come from major world religions, like Christianity, Hinduism and Buddhism. But if you dissect different monk movements and find similarities between them, you will find that their core principles aren't religious in nature at all. [1]

And neither living in a remote monastery nor praying are examples of those core principles. Those are merely implementations of those principles that are specific to a particular religious denomination.

Thinking like a monk is primarily all about deliberately designing your lifestyle rather than just letting daily events randomly happen. It's not just about designing any random type of lifestyle, but doing it in such a way that it will make you the best person you can possibly be in the area of your choice

Religious devotees would isolate themselves in a community of like-minded people away from modern civilization because this would help them reach their goal of becoming as close to their religion's definition of an ideal person as possible. This is the reason why they do the things they do.

But if you take the same core principles that any monk movement uses and apply them to the development of your programming craft and career, then those principles will help you to get yourself as close to excellence as possible in those areas.

Thinking like a monk and designing your lifestyle according to monk-like principles is perhaps the fastest way of developing both the right habits and a growth mindset to realize your full-potential: The best programmer you can be.

So, since you now know that having a monk mentality is not necessarily about wearing funny clothes and praying whole day long, let's have a look at what exactly it is.

What is a monk mentality?

If you completely ignore religion and any other spiritual beliefs, then you will see that different monk movements share a list of just a handful of core principles:

- **Monks live by a routine that is set in stone.** Monks don't have much free time. Their entire day is planned ahead of time. Everything is done according to this routine and there is no deviation from it.

  They have a specific time when they go to bed. They have a specific time when they wake up. They eat their meals at specific times.

- **Monks are constantly working on self-improvement.** Monks dedicate their lives to become what their religion considers to be a perfect person. The shared belief between different monastic movements is that the state of full perfection is impossible to achieve, but it's every monk's duty to get as close to it as possible.

  The specific things that monks do differ depending on the religious denomination they belong to, because different denominations have different definitions of perfection. But the general principle of doing constant self-improvement is applied by all monastic movements.

- **Monks do things in specific prescribed ways.** As a monk, when it's time to eat your meal, you don't just eat it in any way you like. And it's not just about table manners. For example, the Eastern Orthodox monks of Mount Athos eat their meals in silence. [2]

  And this applies to everything that monks do. They sturdy prescribed ritualistic ways of doing everything and they stick to these rules. They walk in a specific way. They pray in a particular way. They sit in a particular way. Everything they do is a ritual.

- **Everything the monks do has a purpose.** People form monastic communities based on shared religious or spiritual beliefs. Those believe systems always include the idea of how to be a perfect human. And every ritual that the monks perform has been explicitly designed to help you to get as close to becoming the best person you can be.

You may not necessarily agree with belief systems of specific monastic communities. You may not even believe that there can be such a thing as a "perfect human". And that's fine too. The core principle of living your life in a purposeful manner is still useful, even if the purpose that you want to fulfil is different from becoming a "perfect human". You can do things for the purpose of achieving the goal of becoming a great programmer.

- **Monks completely eliminate distractions that can prevent them from reaching their goals.** In religion, there are many different taboos. Religions define anything that contradicts their core values as "sinful". But the same thing that are considered sinful are often very tempting (certain foods, sex, gambling, etc.).

  But monastic communities have been designed in such a way that none of these tempting things are present in their lives. And this is precisely why monasteries are normally built in remote places. It's physically hard to deliver anything there that's considered "bad" by the standards of there religion.

  There are also very strict monastery rules that enforce it. The monastic all-male communities of Mount Athos, for example, don't allow any women to visit [2].

  But it's not only remoteness of the monasteries and their strict rules that eliminate all temptations. The fact that monks live by routines that are set in stone also helps. With so many different rituals and duties that they have to follow on a daily basis, monks don't have time to engage in the activities that are contrary to their goals. They don't even have much time to think about those distractions.

As you can see, the core principles of monasticism are not necessarily religious in nature. They can be applied in many different settings

In a nutshell, monk mentality is when someone aims to achieve a particular goal and designs their life in such a way that it only consists of activities that would help the person achieve such a goal. Every activity that doesn't serve this goal is completely eliminated.

Because these principles are consistently practiced in monasteries across the world, adhering to relatively strict schedule for a period of time to focus on a single goal of purposeful self-improvement in a particular area of your life while eliminating as many distractions as possible is often referred to as "monk mode". [3] And making a conscious commitment to adhere to these principles is what we referred to as "monk mentality". Essentially, you adopt the same way of thinking as the monks do, even if you only intend to live by monastic principles temporarily

If you take religious beliefs out, the core principles that monks live by are the same as those used in military boot camps and training camps for elite athletes. These are the principles that help civilians become fully trained soldiers within months rather than years. Likewise, it's the only way to train for elite sporting events, where training and recovery is all you do for a period of time in preparation for your competition event.

What works for elite members of one profession is equally applicable to elite members of another profession. This is why those who aspire to become elite programmers will gain a lot if they will learn to think like a monk and be able to go into the "monk mode", at least, on occasion.

Why programmers should care about what monks do

Unless you are religious or genuinely curious about monasticism, then you wouldn't care much about the exact rituals that the monks perform. And they, obviously, are as far removed from the world of software development as you can imagine.

But it's not the exact rituals–how monks from a particular religious denomination pray and at what time they eat their meals–that you should care about or try to emulate. It's the core principles that all monk movements used to come up with those rituals that's important. With that knowledge as a template you can design the perfect routine for yourself that will help you reach your goals quickly. In fact, monk mentality is probably the thing that will help you to reach your goals the quickest.

If you apply monk mentality in your life, then, just like in a religious monastery, your life will consist of rituals and be devoid of distractions. But those rituals won't be the same as the monks do. It's about coming up with a list of daily routines that will make you a better programmer and actively eliminating all distractions that don't serve this purpose

Implementing core monastic principles

If you are familiar with object-oriented programming paradigm, you will know the concept of *interfaces* and their *implementations*. And it's a perfect analogy to describe how core principles behind monastic movements are applicable to programming

In case you aren't familiar with object-oriented programming, interface is a structure that defines what specific functionality its implementation should have. But it doesn't have any concrete logic defined. The exact logic belongs in a structure that implements the interface, which is usually called *class*.

Those core principles of a monk's life represent an interface. But you have to come up with your own implementation of it to make it applicable to programming. And this is how you can do it:

- **Set your routine in stone.** There are many benefits of having a non-negotiable routine as a programmer. And there aren't any real downsides.

  It's up to you what exact routine you'll come up with. You'll have to perform some trial and error to come up with the perfect routine for yourself. The most optimal type of routine for me probably won't be the most optimal routine for you.

  But in general, your routine needs to consist of those things that will make you a better programmer. For example, you may dedicate specific hours of each day to studying or coding practice. Perhaps you could also dedicate a particular part of a particular day to participating on programming forums. Even your day-to-day job may be split into different types of tasks

- **Dedicate your routine to self-improvement in a specific area.** Another thing you can borrow from monks is the inclusion of deliberate study in your routine. Monks don't merely work on themselves to be better followers of their religion. They regularly study religious texts to gain a better idea of what being a better person means.

  Same applies to you as a programmer. You need to deliberately set aside time for studying best practices. This will not just get you in a habit of writing code, but will allow you to continuously improve the code you write.

- **Perform your tasks in a proper prescribed way.** Monks don't just go through the motions as they go about your day. Every task they are scheduled to complete is done with full dedication and attention. They treat almost everything in their life as a form of religious worship. So, why not treat your programming career as a religion?

  If you adopt a monk mentality, you won't be completing the tasks from your routine just to tick the box. You will be doing every task you've given yourself with full attention. This is where the concept of deep work comes into play.

  But you don't merely work in a focused way. You also perform each task in the best possible way known to you. For example, you shouldn't just produce any solution that solves a particular problem. You will need to come up with the solution that adheres to all best practices known to you, so today's solution won't be a problem tomorrow.

  Edsger W. Dijkstra, a notorious computer scientist, said the following to those who want to excel in software development or scientific research:

  "Raise your quality standards as high as you can live with, avoid wasting your time on routine problems, and always try to work as closely as possible at the boundary of your abilities. Do this, because it is the only way of discovering how that boundary should be moved forward." [4]

- **Everything you include in your routine needs to have a purpose.** Even though the overarching goal of your routine is to become the best programmer you can possibly be, not every programming-related task you come up with will be helpful. Likewise, not every task that's unrelated to programming will be unhelpful.

  A monk-like routine is there to squeeze the maximum out of the time available to you. So you don't include any random tasks that may sound compelling.

  For example, you might be tempted to spend extra time each day studying some old programming language that you will most likely never use in your career. Even though it's a task related to programming, this is not the best use of your time. And this extra work may make you feel burned out.

  On the other hand, having an activity such as a sports session, get-together with your friends or a walk added to your routine may be extremely useful for your career development, as recreational activities will help you recharge, so you are ready to tackle difficult coding problems once again.

  So, your routine doesn't need to consist exclusively of activities that are directly related to programming. But every activity you put in your routine absolutely must have a purpose.

- **Eliminate all distractions to the extent that it's possible.** To some extent, having a set-in-stone routine eliminates distractions. When you wake up in the morning and you know exactly where you need to be next and what you need to do, you are less likely to start randomly browsing the web.

  When you fill your day with routines, there is less time in it for distractions. And if you actually make pre-defined recreational activities a part of your routine, you won't be as tempted to take an unscheduled break for a mindless use of social media.

Other than that, we have already covered in chapters 1, 2 and 3 how you can eliminate distractions that programmers are especially susceptible to. And then, in chapters 4 and 5, we had a look at how to create an echo-chamber around you, which is the closest you can have to being in a community of like-minded people, like monks.

You now have some basic ideas of how to apply monk mentality to a software development career. Now, based on what you already know about how habits work, let's have a look at what will happen if you treat your career as a religion and if you apply a monk-like lifestyle around it.

Designing your routine

If you want to try out the monk mode, there are ways of making it as effective as possible. We will shortly have a look at how you can design an optimal monk-like routine for yourself while eliminating distractions. But first, let's reiterate why a well-designed routine is one of the best tools in your arsenal of self-improvement.

You will improve every day if your routine is consistent

We have covered in chapter 1 how neural pathways in the brain are formed and how repetition is fundamental to their formation. And this is why, if you follow a consistent routine for long enough, you will build strong neural pathways. Those productive activities that you have chosen to make a part of your routine will become habitual.

For example, if you have decided to get up every day at a specific time and then spend the next hour practicing algorithms, this action will eventually become automatic. You won't be thinking about whether or not you should start studying. You will just start studying, because this is what you usually do. It will be a fully automated action.

But doing things according to a monk mentality is not only about routines. It's about trying to do everything in the best way possible. And if doing your tasks as diligently as possible and with as much focus as possible is what you have been consciously trying to do every day, then eventually it will become your default way of working.

And that's how you acquire the right habits to master the craft of programming in the quickest way possible.

It's not a coincidence that the process of mastering a craft often gets compared to techniques that have originally been developed inside monasteries. For example, some mindfulness meditation practices that were originally developed by Buddhist monks are often recommended as a tool for achieving the focus necessary for deep work that we have discussed in chapter 2.

Robert Greene, author of *The 48 Laws of Power*, is a big proponent of mindfulness as a tool for achieving mastery. When he did research for his book called *Mastery*, he studied the literature on Japanese samurai warriors, who were skillful masters of their craft and Zen practitioners. And he said the following about the relationship between mastery and Zen-like intense focus:

> *"The time that leads to mastery is dependent on the intensity of our focus."* [5]

There is nothing that changes your habits and builds your skills quicker than a consistent focused routine without any distractions. This is why people who decide to join a monastery seem to change in seemingly no time at all. Many people are known to have completely gotten rid of various bad habits, like excessive drinking or drug usage, shortly after joining a monastery, while they've struggled to give up these things for years prior to this. [6]

But you don't have to wait until new neural pathways will get established to rip benefits of a monk mentality in action. There are tangible benefits of a monk-like lifestyle that you can take advantage of from day one. One of them is to eliminate indecisiveness from your life and prevent yourself from getting into the state of analysis paralysis.

How to never get into analysis paralysis

Have you ever been in a situation where, even though you vaguely knew what your goals are, you struggled to figure out what to do in a particular moment of time? You saw multiple options, each of which seemed as good as any other.

Shall I work through a coding tutorial, or shall I exercise? Or maybe I should spend some time on my side project?

And then, you end up procrastinating instead of choosing any of these options. Or perhaps you choose a productive activity, but it took you a long time to decide. The precious time you could have spent actually performing the activity was wasted on comparing it against other activities you could have been doing.

This phenomenon is known as "analysis paralysis" [7]. And monk mentality is one of the best ways to overcome it.

If you design a routine for yourself and make it non-negotiable, you won't be thinking about what activity to do next at any given moment of time. Your day will be pre-planned in advance. You will just pick whichever activity you have on your list for the current time period.

You will have dedicated time for planning your routine. And it will be OK to spend as much time as you need to think about what you need to do. It's a time window that has been dedicated specifically for this purpose, so it won't interfere with the actual activities.

This is when you also decide whether or not any specific activity actually provides you benefits. Every activity you put into your routine must have a purpose. You don't want to waste your time on something that doesn't serve you. And you don't want to increase your workload to an extent where it makes you feel burned out. But it's not always instantly obvious what kind of activities would benefit you and what kind of activities wouldn't.

This is why you need to take your time to evaluate what exactly you need to put into your routine. And this is definitely not something you should be doing when you are about to perform an activity.

What kind of activities you should filter out from your routine

When I was starting my career as a software developer, I wanted to be the best I could be. And to do so, initially filled my time with trying to learn low- and medium-level languages, such as C and assembly.

Those are the languages that I never had to use in my career. But I just assumed that, because these languages operate at a lower level than the languages I've been actually using, they would make me understand better how computers work.

Those languages were hard, because they have been intended to be hard. Taking time to study them on top of my day job made me mentally exhausted. But in hindsight, I haven't gained anything beneficial from studying them.

If you use high-level languages, like the majority of software developers do, you don't really need a detailed knowledge of how underlying hardware works. Yes, basic knowledge of the hardware is a must, but basic knowledge won't take you much time to obtain.

However, when you are studying low-level languages, there is a lot to learn. These are the languages where you need to manually manage memory and spend a lot of time optimizing your code.

And if studying medium-level languages, like C or C++, is still somewhat useful, then studying low-level languages, like assembly, is probably a waste of time, unless your actual role involves writing actual assembly code or working with CPU architecture. Low-level languages aren't easily readable by humans. And they don't perform intuitive actions that everyone is familiar with, like basic calculations. Instead, they move chunks of data from one register in a CPU into another. This is so different from how things are done in high-level languages that the knowledge gained studying assembly will not be applicable to your normal area of expertise.

Of course, I'm not saying that you definitely shouldn't attempt to learn assembly if you specialize in high-level languages. If you are genuinely interested in how your high-level language gets compiled into low-level instructions, why not learn it? But for me personally, it was the wrong choice of activity. It took a lot of time and effort without providing any tangible benefits.

Studying assembly is just an example. Software development is a vast field with many niches. It's impossible to learn it all and typically you will occupy a specific niche. But it's easy to get pulled into extracurricular activities that are absolutely irrelevant to your niche.

Programming is hard and studying something new in programming is often even harder. This is why the activities that are intended to improve your programming skills will drain your mental energy. And this is precisely why you need to be careful which extracurricular activities you include in your routine.

Everything you add to your routine must serve a purpose. So, whenever you hear some famous programming blogger or thought leader saying that every single programmer needs to know a particular technology, technique or a language, stop and think. If you can't come up with a clear answer to how knowing this will help you in your specific career-related or other self-improvement goals, then perhaps you should skip it.

When choosing activities for your routine, you should prioritize anything that is directly relevant to your goals. For an aspiring or a current programmer, those could be as follows:

- Coding challenges in the languages you work with.

- More in-depth study of these languages.

- Best practices of using these languages.

For everything else, if you don't see any clear benefit, then skip it. Having a nice walk through the woods would serve you much better than spending time studying a language that you will never use while you are already mentally exhausted.

But for some people, even merely thinking about having a non-negotiable routine may sound overwhelming, even if it only consists of purposeful activities. The good news is, however, that there are additional things you can do to prevent yourself from getting overwhelmed with a routine.

How to not get overwhelmed with routines

One important thing to remember is that a monk-like routine applied to your career development is just a tool. You don't live in an actual monastery and you don't have to abide by arbitrary rules that you aren't comfortable with. So, you are free to design the routine that would suit you.

Monk mode doesn't have to be a dull existence with all work and no play. And neither should your routine consist of only work-related activities.

If you follow a monk lifestyle template fully, then yes, the routine is expected to occupy pretty much all of your time. But the activities you put in it would include recreation as well as work. The only rule that you need to follow is that everything you put into your routine needs to be there for a reason.

So, a properly designed routine will not have a negative effect on your work-life balance. On the contrary, you will have set-in-stone time when you turn your computer off and perform something that is not related to work.

Cal Newport, the author of *Deep Work*, said the following about the importance of having a set-in-stone time when you complete all of your work-related activities:

> *"If you keep interrupting your evening to check and respond to e-mail, or put aside a few hours after dinner to catch up on an approaching deadline, you're robbing your directed attention centers of the uninterrupted rest they need for restoration. Even if these work dashes consume only a small amount of time, they prevent you from reaching the levels of deeper relaxation in which attention restoration can occur. Only the confidence that you're done with work until the next day can convince your brain to downshift to the level where it can begin to recharge for the next day to follow. Put another way, trying to squeeze a little more work out of your evenings might reduce your effectiveness the next day enough that you end up getting less done than if you had instead respected a shutdown." [8]*

Recreation isn't a waste of time. It's actually a tool to make you more effective at your work. To use a metaphor from a gym, your muscles grow when you rest, not when you train. And the same applies to any other area of work, whether it's physical or intellectual.

But there is a big advantage of specifically writing recreational activities into your schedule. Just like with work-related tasks, you will minimize the analysis paralysis while having a break. And you will do something that is truly fulfilling and restorative instead of mindlessly browsing the web and binge-watching silly videos.

Plus, you don't have to follow a strict routine for the whole duration of the day. Perhaps you will choose to only have a strict schedule during the working hours and then you will make your evenings free to do things spontaneously. After all, a monk-like routine is merely a suggestion and not a prescription that will suit everyone.

Also, when you start designing a routine for yourself, you may not come up with a perfect one straight away. And this is OK too. Any time you feel like you are overwhelmed and are about to burn out, you can reduce the number of work-related activities in your schedule. Likewise, if the routine feels too light, you can add some more activities to it. Or you may modify your routine after a couple of weeks, as it will only become apparent then that some of the activities don't actually serve you well.

Lastly, you shouldn't worry if, for whatever reason, you can't keep up with the schedule you've set up for yourself. Sometimes things get out of our control. Unexpected events happen. Other times, we underestimate how long specific tasks take to complete.

But it's not a problem. Cal Newport, in his book *Deep Work*, described a technique that he personally uses to mitigate against unforeseen circumstances.

He actually follows a very similar system himself. He plans his every day and he tracks time spent on each activity. But when unforeseen circumstances happen, he simply adjusts the remainder of his schedule on the spot, perhaps by removing lower-priority items from it. **[8]**

Tasks that are both urgent and important always take priority. But not everything in your schedule is both urgent and important. The self-improvement tasks that you have assigned for yourself will, without a doubt, deliver great benefits to you in the future, so they are important. But they are nowhere near as urgent as your current work-related obligations. Therefore, if you find that you can't complete all the tasks you have originally placed in your schedule, focus on your most urgent obligations first. Leave them in your schedule. Then, prioritize the remaining tasks based on their importance. Start removing (or moving back) tasks with lesser importance.

So, in a nutshell, the monk-style routine you will design for yourself won't be overwhelming. It will be as strict or as flexible as you are comfortable with. And it's absolutely OK to not get your routine right the first time. But, as you can probably see by now, following a well-structured routine while aggressively eliminating distractions is perhaps the most efficient way of achieving both your short-term and long-term goals.

But it's not only that living like a monk is not overwhelming. When you design an optimal monk-like lifestyle for yourself, you will actually start to enjoy it. And you won't want to go back.

Why a properly designed monk-like routine will feel good

One thing to remember about monastic movements is that people join them willingly. And they rarely want to go back. Usually, even if they do return into normal society, they still retain many lifestyle elements from their former monk life. [9]

So there must be something about the monk lifestyle that is enjoyable. And there indeed is.

First of all, a well-structured life increases simplicity, which, in turn, reduces anxiety. Being in a state of indecision is not pleasant. You may feel anxious when you are aware that there are many things that require your attention, but you don't know where they stand in terms of priority. But if you decide ahead of time what exactly you need to do and when, your anxiety is reduced.

This simplicity is not only brought about by the things that you have included in your schedule, but the distracting things you no longer have access to because of how you've designed your schedule. You no longer have time for highly addictive mindless activities that drain a lot of your brain power, like aimless social media usage we have discussed in chapter 3.

Then there is the feeling of accomplishment from all the work you are able to complete within a much shorter period of time than before. If you dedicate a specific period of time to productive activities and make them non-negotiable, then you will achieve more than someone who performs his tasks in an ad-hoc fashion.

Then there is the state of flow, which will be easier to enter when you dedicate enough time to activities that are conducive to it. In chapter 2, we have already discussed why the state of flow is a pleasurable state to be in. And this mental state is, in fact, what real monks experience on a regular basis. Perhaps, they don't use the same terminology and call it "zen" or "grace", depending on their religious background. But when they talk about it, it closely matches the description of the state of flow. [9]

Finally, your work-life balance will also improve. Having a rule of stopping all of your work-related activities at a particular time will give you more time to spend with your friends and family or to perform the hobbies that you enjoy. Likewise, restricting your work time to only specific hours will make it easier for you to give productive activities your full focus.

So, there is a lot to gain from adopting a monk-like lifestyle and nothing to lose. The quality of your life will improve. The only caveat is that it may take some time for you to come up with your own routine. But it's well worth it.

So, you may be wondering by now, what kind of a routine should you design for yourself that will specifically aid you in the goal of becoming an excellent software developer? Well, as I've mentioned, your routine must be your own. But I will give you an example of a routine that I've used, so you can use it as a template.

Example routine you can use

There are certain rules that I used while designing a routine for myself. For me personally, as well as being a good software developer, it's important for me to be physically strong and fit. So, my personal routine must include physical exercises.

Likewise, as well as aspiring to be a quality programmer, I also aspire to help as many aspiring programmers as possible to fulfill their potential. This is why my routine must include the activities such as writing blog posts, publishing video lectures or mentoring someone.

Another important thing to take into consideration is your current environment. For example, my routine during ordinary times would be much more flexible than it was during, for example, a global COVID-19 pandemic, when most of the countries had severe restrictions on what people could and couldn't do. As I found out, filling time with set-in-stone activities during a prolonged period of a monotonous lockdown actually makes the lockdown much more tolerable.

So, the first thing I do while designing my routine is deciding which activities I absolutely must accomplish during each week. After doing some trial and error, I came up with the following list (which excludes my work-related activities as a developer):

- Complete at least one coding challenge.

- Read at least one article about programming best practices.

- Get up to date with the news in tech.

- Write a blog article or film an educational video lecture about programming. Alternatively, mentor someone or participate in discussions or Q&A sessions on programming forums.

- Read at least one of my own previously published blog posts.

- Have at least three strength-training sessions.

- Have at least one running session.

And then, based on this, my typical working day may look something like this:

6:00 - Wake up

6:00 - 7:30 - Strength training (including commute and shower)

7:30 - 8:00 - Breakfast

8:00 - 9:30 - Writing a blog post

9:30 - 12:00 - Work

12:00 - 13:00 - Lunch

13:00 - 18:00 - Work

18:00 - 19:00 - Dinner

19:00 - 21:00 - Family activities

21:00 - 22:00 - Reading

In this sample schedule, I've put two sections that I have labeled "work". But in my actual schedule, I split them up even further. I give a separate time slot for every scheduled meeting. And I dedicate specific time slots for specific work-related tasks.

Seeing your work as a collection of microtasks is a very effective way of tricking your brain into being able to complete a high volume of it. And this is what we will discuss in chapter 8.

Of course, while designing a work-related schedule, one has to consider other work-related obligations, like regular meetings. The time slots dedicated to those meetings are occupied, so you can't schedule anything else in. But meetings do occasionally finish early, so it may be a good practice to tentatively add some less urgent tasks into these time slots in case this happens. I have been doing this on a regular basis. This way, I have been able to squeeze some additional productive activity into my schedule now and again.

Occasionally, if unforeseen circumstances happen or if my original estimation wasn't accurate enough, I move the time slots. It also happens that I end up never actually doing some of the less important tasks that I have originally planned to complete. There are even days when urgent work-related deadlines come and I don't manage to achieve anything other than specific work-related obligations. But still, having this system in place allows me to achieve much more than I would have been able to.

Timeless technique proven by monks, athletes and elite soldiers

It's not only monks that have specific routines, are forced to perform things to high standards and eliminate distractions from their environment. This is the lifestyle that has been practiced since the dawn of time by representatives of professions that were considered to be "elite", whether it's elite soldiers, athletes or statespeople.

All elite professions always had and always will have a strict code that they live by. And it only differs from the monastic lifestyle by implementation details. The core principles of it are the same.

It's not even clear whether monastic movements were the ones who originally came up with the lifestyle based on these principles. And neither is it important. All that matters is that these principles work, as has been proven many times throughout the centuries by representatives of pretty much any elite profession.

So, if you want to become an elite programmer, why not give a try to the system that worked so well for other elite professions? It worked well for the other elite professions and now you know why it will work for you as a programmer.

We have now covered various ways of how you can build a growth mindset, create a positive echo chamber, and start seeing things from the perspective of someone who wants to be a top level programmer. Next, we will move on to specific techniques that will make your daily programming activities easier and more enjoyable. The following chapters will cover each of those techniques in detail, but you can also download a summary of these techniques, along with some other productivity hacks, from here: https://simpleprogrammer. com/10hacks/

Whether you choose to try the monk mode or not, as a professional programmer, you will have to have hours-long time slots in your schedule dedicated to your work, as you have already seen in the example of a monk-like routine. Also, it's inevitable that you will have to face large chunks of work that will take you days to complete. But there is a planning trick you can use to make these long periods of continuous work seem much shorter than they are. And those large and hard tasks will seem much smaller and easier.

In the next chapter, we will cover the concept of microtasks. You will learn why splitting a big chunk of work into atomic micro-activities will make the activity much easier to complete, even when the actual amount of work doesn't change. When you start applying this technique, you will start seeing that you can accomplish more within a shorter time. And your ability to focus on your work will improve too.

Microtasks will compliment your monk-like routine perfectly. Just like the routine itself, they are also extremely effective at eliminating analysis paralysis. Only that they are much more fine-grained than the monk mode routine itself.

References

1. Jey Shetty - Think Like a Monk: The secret of how to harness the power of positivity and be happy now - Thorsons
2. Father Spyridon Bailey - Journey to Mount Athos - FeedaRead.com
3. Mésac Adna - Monk Mode: Be More By Doing Less -
4. Edsger W. Dijkstra - Selected Writings on Computing: A personal Perspective - Springer
5. Robert Greene - Mastery - Profile Books
6. Rowan Williams - The Way of St Benedict - Bloomsbury Continuum
7. Dan Smith - Mental Focus: How to Overcome Analysis Paralysis
8. Cal Newport - Deep Work: Rules for Focused Success in a Distracted World - Piatkus
9. Br. Benet Tvedten - How to Be a Monastic and Not Leave Your Day Job: An Invitation to Oblate Life - Paraclete Press

CHAPTER 8

DEFEATING PROCRASTINATION WITH MICROTASKS

When eating an elephant, take one bite at a time.

-- *Creighton Abrams*

Every programmer, myself included, occasionally feels a strong urge to procrastinate. Unfortunately, there is no getting away from it.

Programming might be something that you have always wanted to do. Perhaps, coding is something you can't stop thinking about whenever you are doing something else. But once you open your laptop to write some code, you don't want to do it anymore. You want to browse some YouTube videos instead. Does it sound familiar?

As we have already covered in chapters 1 and 2, it is completely normal to want to procrastinate when you are faced with a challenging task. Even if you have developed the right habits, have built a productive mindset, and have established ideal routines, the desire to procrastinate would still occasionally pop up. But the good news is that there is a very effective technique to defeat such an urge, which we will talk about shortly.

Perhaps the urge to procrastinate every time you try to do some work will even make you believe that you have completely lost your passion for the craft you used to love so much. But it probably isn't the case.

Yes, the desire to procrastinate might even increase over time, but this won't necessarily be because you lost your passion. As you already know from chapter 1, procrastination is the brain's defense mechanism against excessive energy expenditure. As you may recall, the human brain, while only occupying around 2% of body weight, uses up to a quarter of its energy.

Even though energy is easy to access these days, this wasn't always the case. The human brain didn't evolve in the period of plenty that we live in now. It evolved in the period of scarcity when individuals didn't know where their next meal was coming from. Therefore, your brain operates as if you still live in such an austere age.

So, the most likely reason why you are feeling the urge to procrastinate is because the task that you are facing is perceived by your subconscious as something excessively big and energy consuming. And the reason why the urge to procrastinate might actually get worse over time is because, as you grow in your career, you take on more and more responsibility.

So, you can now see that the fact that you are feeling an urge to procrastinate more often might not be because you fell out of love with the craft of programming. It might actually be an indicator that your career is going in the right direction and that you are becoming more valuable as a professional.

But fortunately, there is a very effective tool for overcoming the urge to procrastinate. Let me introduce you to the concept of microtasks.

Why microtasks trick your brain to not procrastinate

There is a popular phrase, variations of which were quoted by many famous people, including general Creighton Abrams and archbishop Desmond Tutu:

> *"When eating an elephant, take one bite at a time."* *[1]*

And, of course, these people are not talking about consuming a large animal for dinner. They are talking about splitting a large task into smaller, much more manageable chunks. And this is what the concept of microtasks is all about.

It's something that you, as a programmer, might be vaguely familiar with already. Perhaps you have already heard suggestions that, if you want to be a polyglot or a full-stack developer, you should focus on learning only one technology at a time. For example, aspiring full-stack developers, whose future job would be to work with both front-end and back-end components of a web application, might be told that they shouldn't try to learn both client- and server-side technologies at the same time. Instead, they should focus on only one. [2]

But this advice doesn't go far enough. Learning all technologies involved just in the front-end is still an enormous task. And it will still put many people off.

The concept of microtasks goes even further. It's about splitting your work into tiny atomic chunks. Preferably, you want to split your task in such a way that you cannot split it any further.

In the above example, instead of trying to learn HTML, JavaScript, CSS and other front-end technologies from scratch, you can define micro-goals for yourself. For example, it might be something as follows:

1. Create a page with the most basic HTML layout.

2. Add the title to the page.

3. Find out how to host it, so you can open it in the browser.

4. Add navigation tabs.

5. Make the tables clickable.

6. Add a picture below the title.

7. Add text below the picture.

8. Add a side panel.

9. Add cards to the side panel.

10. Apply CSS to your page to make it look acceptably nice.

11. Add some JavaScript that opens a pop-up dialog when you click some component on the page.

Once you've done this, getting to start on your task becomes incredibly easy. You need to temporarily forget about the bigger picture and simply focus on the current task. And the task would be so small that even if you had a strong habit of procrastinating or an urge to, it would be relatively easy to overcome. Your brain would simply tell you: "Sure! I can do this one small thing!"

How to use microtasks most effectively

Just like with any tools, there are ways of getting the most out of microtasks. And if you use it specifically to defeat the urge to procrastinate, the best way to deal with microtasks is to just focus on a single task ahead and allow yourself to have a break once it's done.

If you view your list of microtasks as something you still need to complete as soon as possible to achieve a bigger goal, your brain may still perceive it as one big task. Sure, the urge to procrastinate will still be weakened, as you already have an outline of the exact steps. But, nonetheless, those are the steps to complete a big chunk of work.

Instead, imagine that the small atomic task that you are dealing with now is the only thing that exists in the universe. All you need to do is complete it. And then, once it's done, you are fully entitled to have some rest or do something fun.

Of course, you don't actually have to stop once you complete a single task. You will probably be able to convince yourself to complete the next task in the same way you've completed the first one. And then the next one. And so on. But the point here is to keep telling yourself that you absolutely can rest once you feel the need to do so after the task is done.

Remember that we are tricking our brain here. So, our brain will reply along the lines of: "There is not much work to do at all. Of course, I can get this done and over with! And then I can do something fun!". And then, once this chunk of work is done, we do it again, so our brain can, metaphorically speaking, produce the same reply.

But it's also important to fulfill this promise that you give yourself. If you do feel a genuine urge to rest after completing any one of your tasks, do so. You don't want to carry on forcing yourself to work when every fiber of your body fights against it. Otherwise, you are in danger of building a negative cue around the microtasks. Your brain will learn to associate them with hard work, so you will no longer be able to utilize them as effectively.

But if you do fulfil your promise to yourself and have a break when you feel like it, then you will build even stronger associations between microtasks and easy work that doesn't consume such energy. When you then give a promise to yourself that you can have a rest if you feel like it once the task at hand is done, your subconscious mind will believe you.

But there is more to microtasks than merely being a trick to defeat procrastination. It's also one of the best tools to enter the productive state of flow.

When you know exactly where to start on your next task and you have a series of concrete steps in front of you, magic can happen once you start working through those steps. Once you have completed a number of microtasks, you may no longer keep convincing yourself that you can have a break after completing just one more. You may enter the state of flow. Once here, you no longer need to keep thinking about how to split the remainder of your task into microtasks.

As you may recall from our discussion in chapter two, it takes around 15 minutes of continuous sustained focus to enter the state of flow. And you are more likely to enter the state of flow if you spend this time actually focusing on something productive rather than forcing yourself to maintain the focus while you are fighting the temptation to procrastinate.

When you split a larger task into a collection of atomic microtasks, you will end up with a series of logical consecutive steps. The completion of one microtask will enable you to start working on the next. The process feels like a natural flow from point A to point B. And this is precisely why doing things this way is very conducive to entering the mental state of flow, where you just get lost in your work.

In fact, once you are in the flow, you don't have to keep using microtasks at all. At this point, you are fully immersed in your work.

You know exactly what you need to do next. And, while you are in this state, there is no longer any urge to procrastinate.

At this point, the main purpose of the microtasks has been fulfilled. And now you are in different mental territory, where microtasks are no longer the best tool for the job. Instead, just let the state of flow take you where you need to be. And just keep on following your instincts while it lasts.

But you can't be in the state of flow 100% of the time. And while working through microtasks is one of the best ways of entering this sought-after mental state of high productivity, there is still no guarantee that you will enter it every single time.

Regardless of whether you do enter the state of flow or not, microtasks will increase your productivity by themselves, as we have already established. But there is one addition to microtasks that you can apply to greatly increase their usefulness.

There are many types of tools that can be made more effective when they are combined with other tools. As a tool, microtasks are not different. To make them even more effective at eliminating procrastination, you can combine them with the concept of pre-planning.

How pre-planning your microtasks make them more effective

Splitting a large chunk of work just before you are about to do it is good. But it's even better if you do it well in advance of starting the said chunk of work. And this is what pre-planning is all about.

One problem with microtasks on their own is that, when you think about how to split your work, it's not always obvious where to start. And, due to this uncertainty, that in itself may be perceived by your brain as hard work–a perfect recipe for procrastination.

But if you have planned your tasks ahead of your work, it's different. You know exactly where to start. You see the exact task ahead of you. And yet there is another important benefit of pre-planning: the creation of productive momentum for your day.

Jocko Willink, the former Navy SEAL whom we've spoken about in chapter 6, has spoken about the critical importance of momentum while trying to maintain discipline. Based on his personal experience, he doesn't believe that willpower is a finite resource. He believes that, as long as you carry on engaging in activities that require discipline, you can maintain the discipline whole day long. And, according to him, the easiest way to maintain the momentum is just to never stop.

In his book, Discipline Equals Freedom, he said the following:

> *"Hesitation allows the moment to pass, the opportunity to be lost, the enemy to get the upper hand. Hesitation turns into cowardice. It stops us from moving forward, from taking initiative, from executing what we know we must. Hesitation defeats us. So we must defeat it." [3]*

He makes a point by waking up at or before 5 AM every single day to hit the gym. And he posts a picture of his wristwatch on social media every morning to motivate his followers.

Another notable Navy SEAL, Admiral William McRaven, held a famous talk at the University of Texas graduation ceremony, where he emphasized the importance of making your bed every morning. [4]

There is nothing special in the act of waking up early and going to the gym or making sure that your bed is made. But it's a little win, which, when done first thing in the morning, sets the right momentum for the rest of the day.

When you do something productive right at the start of your day, it's then easy to move onto another productive task. However, if you start your day by pressing the "snooze" button on your alarm or browsing social media, it then becomes hard to start something productive. There is a friction in the form of context switching, which we have covered in chapter 2.

And this is where pre-planning comes into play. If you pre-plan the list of your tasks before your workday even starts, you'll minimize the friction. At this point, you know exactly what you need to do. You can ease yourself into the productive mode, even if your brain hasn't fully awakened yet, just by doing something productive straight away. And that's how you generate productive momentum.

How to pre-plan effectively

To utilize the tool of pre-planning to its maximum potential, you need to get into the habit of not leaving your work for the day until you have created the plan for the next day. This way, you will always know exactly what to do when you start your day.

As a software developer who worked in an agile environment, you will probably be familiar with the concepts of Kanban and Sprint. For those of you who aren't familiar with the terms, roughly speaking, Sprint is a list of tasks that a software development team has planned to do within a fixed period of time. Kanban, on the other hand, is a continuous list of tasks that need to be completed in the order of priority. And you can treat your pre-planned list of microtasks as mini-Kanban or mini-Sprint.

There is also another important principle to follow. While coming up with the list of microtasks for a day, it's always better to over-estimate than under-estimate.

Switching between doing work and planning is a context switch. And just like any other context switch, it consumes mental energy. But it's not a big problem when you are switching into the planning mode while all work for the day has already been completed. After all, you won't have to maintain focus afterwards. But it may become a problem if your day is interrupted by having to come up with a plan.

So, if you under-estimate the amount of work that you can complete in a day, you may end up in the situation where you've completed it all by mid-day. And then you'll have to come up with a list of things to do next. That's one context switch. Then, you are back into working mode. That's context switch number two.

But when you overestimate the amount of work, you may be able to spend the whole day in the productive working mode. And then, you may not even have to plan for the following day. You will just continue from where you've left off. And the flow of tasks will still be fresh in your mind.

And there is another good reason why pre-planning is best to be done at the end of your working day, beyond minimizing the amount of context switching. This is when you have used up a lot of your mental energy, so it won't be wise to start on any new tasks. Because of this, the planning session won't be interfering with your work.

Also, it's a good way to draw a boundary around your working day. If you do it regularly, your brain will start recognizing it as a cue that no more work is to be done today. And your sleep won't be interrupted by the thoughts about your work either, as it happens to many software developers.

There won't be anything to think about. Everything that was in your head has already been transferred to paper. And you'll know that everything that's written on that piece of paper is intended to be read and thought about tomorrow. But for the rest of today, you can rest.

But, as a developer, you know that not every task functions this way. Sometimes you can't pre-plan what exact steps you'll split it into. It happens that you may don't know what to do next until you have partially completed the task.

But this is not a problem. Pre-planning is there primarily to create the right kind of momentum. Your plan doesn't have to be perfect.

Why you shouldn't worry about making a perfect plan

Whether or not you split your work into microtasks ahead of time. it's the same amount of work that needs to be done. But if you do this it will be much easier for you to jump right into work. And that's what microtask and pre-planning are for–to minimize friction.

Pre-planning isn't there to come up with the perfect plan to follow for the rest of your day. But it's there to give you the starting point to leap into a productive mode and gather momentum.

In many programming problems, it's impossible to know ahead of time what specific steps of the solution will be. You need to partially solve the problem to get such clarity. And this should be reflected in pre-planning.

When you are pre-planning, the only steps that need to be accurately defined are the next steps that you will be working on. As a programmer, you will be in position to see these steps. This way, the process of pre-planning will fulfill its purpose. You will know exactly what to do. You will be able to jump into your work right away without thinking about it too much.

But those are the only steps that need to be set in stone. Any remaining steps should be treated as something that may change if needed. Then, your plan gets adjusted organically as you work through your microtasks and gain more clarity on what to do next.

You shouldn't try to have a separate planning session whenever you need to adjust your plan. You already know that switching between two different types of work, e.g., programming and planning, is a context switch. And every context switch drains your mental energy.

What you should do instead is adjust your plan as soon as you have an idea on how the workflow should be adjusted. These ideas will just appear organically as you complete chunks of your work. Completion of certain steps gives you more clarity of what needs to be done next. And that's where these ideas come from.

So, when you see that there are better steps that you need to perform than the ones you have previously written on your plan, just change the next couple of steps on your plan right away. This way, you aren't switching between two different types of work. You are merely writing down the ideas that have organically appeared in your head. And then, if you don't feel like taking a break yet, just carry on working on these steps.

Essentially, the difference between adjusting the steps of your plan organically and having a dedicated planning session to make the adjustments to you plan is that the former consists of the following steps:

1. You work through the list of the microtasks.

2. After completing some items, you see that you can change some microtasks ahead of you.

3. While this thought is still in your head, you go ahead and change only these specific steps.

4. You carry on working through the steps as normal.

You don't stop to re-plan. You make targeted adjustments while you are carrying on with your work.

Another reason why you shouldn't worry about making a perfect plan is because, if you happen to enter the state of flow, you'll be able to forget about your plan altogether for the time being. In this state, you will be fully immersed in your work. And you will know what to do next without having to look at a piece of paper or a spreadsheet for guidance.

A pre-planned list of microtasks exist for two very specific reasons:

1. To make it easy not to procrastinate.

2. To know exactly what to do next if you get interrupted.

If your plan serves these two purposes, then it is a perfect plan already. Don't worry about having to adjust your plan as you work through it.

But there are some tricks you can do to minimize the amounts of adjustments you have to make along the way. So, let's talk about the most optimal structure of your list of microservices.

How to structure microtasks for the best effect

Ideally, each of your microtasks needs to represent a single atomic functionality, which means that it should be so small that there will be no point of splitting it anymore.

Of course, it still needs to represent a meaningful piece of work and still needs to be large enough to make you feel that you've accomplished something once you've completed the task. So, writing a single line of code would be too small to represent a meaningful microtask, while writing a single function may be just the right scope for a microtask

There is no hard and fast rule on how big or small a single microtask should be. There are just two principles you need to adhere to:

1. It needs to represent a meaningful atomic chunk of work, splitting which any further would not produce any additional value.

2. It needs to be small enough that your brain perceives it as easy.

When you are pre-planning a list of microtasks for yourself to go through, sometimes it would be possible to split your entire workload into well-defined microtasks in advance. For example, you may be working on a feature where you need to write a UI based on some wireframes that have already been drawn. This UI needs to rely on data stored in a database. And there needs to be some server-side back-end code which facilitates the communication between the front-end UI and the database.

In this case, you may know exactly what to do. The only issue is that this work will take time. So, in this situation, you will be able to define all required microtasks from start to finish. However, as we have discussed before, programmers often deal with situations where the full list of concrete steps to produce a solution is impossible to know ahead of time.

Programming is not only about writing boilerplate code and applying standard solutions to standard problems. Programming often involves research.

For example, you may have read somewhere that a particular technology, which may be a language, a framework, or a library, is the best tool to solve a particular type of a problem. Now, you are facing a problem of exactly this kind. But you have never used this technology before. You need to evaluate its suitability and produce a proof of concept before you can even start to apply it as the solution.

As someone who has never used such a technology, you can't possibly know all the steps that you need to complete to come up with a suitable solution. Before you are in the position to do so, you need to get familiar with the technology.

196

In this situation, you will be able to outline the exact steps to get started and turn them into microtasks. But you will still have a vague idea where to go next after you've completed these steps.

So, in this case, the best way to plan is to define as many concrete microtasks that will cover the beginning of the process. But for the rest of the process, just outline some vague chunks of work that you can turn into concrete microtasks later. This way, you will not have to do much re-planning at all once you progress through your task and gain more clarity on what you need to do next. You will just be splitting existing items into smaller chunks, which is easier.

If you are familiar with distributed application development and microservices architecture, you'll find this principle of planning to be similar to the monolith-first approach while defining application architecture. If you apply this approach, you start with a large application, known as a "monolith". And then, as you iteratively develop it and it becomes clearer to you which parts of the application can be isolated, you split it into separate microservices. [5] When applied to planning your workload, it's the same principle, but it will be programming tasks that you split into smaller atomic chunks rather than a software application.

Now, as you know how to efficiently pre-plan your microtasks, let's have a look at some examples of standard software development work and decide which of them would meet the criteria to be defined as microtasks.

What would represent a microtask and what wouldn't?

Here are some examples of tasks that software developers get involved in on a regular basis:

- Writing front-end for a distributed application.

- Adding a component to a user interface.

- Writing a microservice inside a distributed application.

- Defining an interface for one of your classes.

- Writing a function or a method.

- Writing a unit test.

- Defining a database schema.

Let's have a look at each one of them in turn and see if it can or cannot be classed as a microtask.

Writing front-end for a distributed application

In a professional-grade software application, the front-end, or the user interface, will be relatively large and complex application components that will take a qualified front-end specialist, or a full-stack developer, days, if not weeks, to do. Therefore, it definitely cannot be classed as a microtask.

However, there might be some exceptions to this. For example, the user interface you are developing might be something very simple that is only intended to be used by the internal user. Perhaps it's nothing more than a status screen for a single process. Or maybe it's a very basic web form. Or maybe this UI is merely a visualization for web API endpoints available in a web application, for which standard libraries would already exist. In any of these situations, creating a UI would be a microtask in and of itself.

But those examples are indeed merely exceptions. In most of the cases, even the internal users will need something relatively complex, even if it doesn't necessarily have to look the best. For example, users may want to see an entire dashboard of various statuses rather than information about a single metric.

Therefore, if your task is to create a front-end, you should probably be able to split it into microtasks. In this case, the best way to do so would be to decide which form components of the user interface can be added separately from each other. Also, defining the markup, applying styling to it, and adding any JavaScript should almost certainly be separate tasks.

Adding a component to a user interface

We have already established that a task of adding a component to a user interface can be a good candidate to be a distinct microtask. But there are caveats. It depends on how big or small this component is.

If the component in question may be just a textbox in a form, then it's too small to be a distinct microtask. It may be just a single HTML element, which is equivalent to a single line of code. But the layout of the whole form, without specific styling and JavaScript-based logic, would probably be a good candidate to be a microtask. It's still a reasonably small task, but it's also a meaningful chunk of functionality.

Other components may be too big to be done within the scope of a single microtask. It could, for example, be UI within a UI. Or maybe it's indeed a single button, but it requires some fairly complex custom styling and animation.

There is no hard and fast rule on how to split UI work, as different user interfaces have different requirements. But, as a rule of thumb, if you anticipate that a chunk of work will take you more than half an hour, you can probably split it into smaller chunks.

Writing a microservice inside a distributed application

Just like a user interface, a microservice inside a distributed application will be written as if it's a separate application in and of itself. As well as defining all its moving parts (classes, interfaces, communication mechanisms, APIs, etc.), you would also need to perform other auxiliary tasks around it, which would include writing unit tests, creating a continuous integration pipeline, creating release notes, etc.

Writing a microservice is never an atomic task. And, if you do it according to best practices and don't neglect things like automated tests, it will take, a microservice would take a while to complete. Therefore, it can never be completed within the scope of a single microtask.

Defining an interface for one of your classes

In object-oriented programming, an interface is a type of object that has a list of accessible fields, properties, and functions (aka methods) that a particular functional object, like a class or a struct, needs to have. An interface would never have any implementation details or any other type of logic. It will only specify names of the functional members, the data types that they return and any parameters that they accept.

Whether or not this can be defined as a microtask would depend on the complexity of the interface. Creating an interface would never be too big of a task to fit the scope of a microservice. But sometimes, it may be too small.

If you are defining an interface with only a handful of definitions and you already know how those are going to be implemented, then perhaps the task of writing the interface would be too small to be moved into a separate unit of work. It will probably take you just a couple of minutes to do.

However, if you need to think about the structure of your interface, then it definitely fits the scope of a microtask.

Writing a function or a method

This is similar in principle to defining an interface. It depends on how complex it is.

The function that you are about to write might be performing some very basic calculation or simply returning some value that it has retrieved from the data storage. In this case, it's too simple and too small to be separated into a distinct unit of work.

But you will also be writing functions that have relatively complex relationships with various dependencies and/or perform relatively complex calculations. In this case, you will also need to be mindful of best practices. For example, you will need to think how to split your function into multiple functions to make sure that it still adheres to the single responsibility principle. In this case, it's definitely a good candidate to be classed as an atomic microtask.

Writing a unit test

This, again, will depend on the complexity of the test.

If you are adhering to strict test-driven development (TDD) principle, then you need to spend a lot of time thinking about your test coverage before you even start writing the actual code. In this case, each individual test could definitely be classed as a separate microtask.

Same applies if you don't follow TDD to the letter, but you still need to write a test to validate a relatively complex unit of behavior. In this case, you will still have to do some thinking. And a single test would still be a substantial unit of work.

But sometimes you need to write a bunch of very simple tests simply to make sure that you have sufficient test coverage. Not every part of your application is complex. And simple units of behavior don't need anything more than a simple test. In this case, it would be better to assign multiple tests to a single microtask.

Defining a database schema

When you are defining a database schema, you aren't writing database creation scripts yet. You are simply drafting a top-level design of your future database and the relationships between its tables.

In most cases, defining the schema can be classed as a distinct microtask. However, sometimes you will have to design a database with some complex relationships.

Perhaps, you will need to develop your database schema iteratively. In some situations, you will need to normalize your initial design to ensure the most efficient data storage. In other cases, you do the opposite. You de-normalize the schema to improve the database performance. [6]

So, while outlining a database schema, if you are confident that you can do it in one relatively short iteration–then schema design should be a single microtask. Otherwise, try to see how many iterations you will have to do it in. Each one of them will be a microtask of its own.

If it's a large schema with many tables, perhaps each of your microtask will focus on outlining a couple of inter-related tables and their relationships.

These were some generic examples of everyday tasks that developers regularly deal with. Next, we will have a look at a specific example of how microtasks were applied in real life.

Real-life microtasks example

As a programmer, I have been regularly pre-planning my work and splitting it into microtasks before I would start coding. A good example of this was where I needed to develop an application that was capable of playing audio on both Windows and Linux.

The company I was employed by at the time was working on hardware and software information systems for railway stations. I was tasked with developing software that would play audio announcements at station's platforms.

The software would be a part of our Internet of Things (IoT) suite and it would be installed on single-board computers that were running Linux. However, we, as software developers in that organization, used Windows on the computers that we were writing software on. Because of this, the software needed to be written in such a way that it would be able to work on both Windows and Linux.

We also had another constraint as developers. The technology stack we worked with was Microsoft .NET. This is what every one of our developers was experienced in. Therefore, as a policy, we weren't allowed to use any alternative technology stack unless we were 100% sure that any particular piece of functionality couldn't be done on .NET.

At the time, I had absolutely no idea how to write an app that could play audio. And on top of that, I had never used Linux prior to being given this task. So, to me, this task seemed enormous. And my instinct was just to put it off.

But I ignored this instinct. I already knew at the time that .NET Core, a variant of the .NET platform, would work on both Windows and Linux. So, I came up with a plan. I split my initial workload into the following parts:

- Compile a list of existing libraries that could play audio on .NET Core regardless of the operating system it runs on.

- For each library, assess its suitability for the project at hand (this would be treated as a separate task for each library).

- If no suitable libraries are found, compile a new list of tasks.

This was more than enough to get started. And it didn't feel like an enormous task anymore. So, I jumped straight in.

Unfortunately, I didn't succeed at the first attempt. Although I managed to find a couple of existing libraries that enabled .NET Core applications to play audio, none of them were suitable for the project. Every one I examined either only worked on one operating system, relied on components that needed to be compiled separately or relied on expensive paid-for components.

So, I got back to the drawing board. And here was my new list of microtasks:

- Find another free cross-platform technology that has either in-built audio playback capabilities or reliable third-party libraries available.

- Investigate how this technology can be integrated with .NET Core.

- Implement the logic in my own app.

- Test the app on Windows.

- Test the app on Linux.

- Finalize the application.

It didn't take me long to complete the first task. I already knew that Node.js, a JavaScript-based programming platform, could run on any operating system. And it was a popular choice for IoT developers. So I started with that.

And I didn't have to look elsewhere. The platform already had a couple of libraries that could play audio regardless of the operating system it was running on. And it was relatively easy to set up.

Luckily, the second item didn't take me long to complete either. .NET Core already had an in-built library that provided integration between compiled .NET code and Node.js applications.

After testing this technology on both Linux and Windows and hearing playback on both, I refactored the application to make it shippable. And I adhered to the company's policy by having most of the application's logic written on .NET and only those components that were absolutely essential for audio playback written on Node.js.

The task that only a few days ago seemed impossible was now done, the requirements were met and my boss was happy.

Eventually, I had a look at the original code in the Node.js library that I had been using and I rewrote the entire application, so it was pure .NET. But that was a different task.

Personally, I give credit to microtasks for helping me complete a lot of my work that would have otherwise taken a lot longer to complete or wouldn't have been completed at all. But microtasks are just a tool. And just like any other tool, it's not necessarily the best fit for every single situation.

When microtasks and pre-planning might be a hindrance

Let's recall that the primary reason for splitting your work into microtasks is to trick your brain to think that the work you are about to do is much smaller and easier, so your subconscious mind would not try to sabotage your efforts to get it done. And the main reason for pre-planning your microtasks in advance is so that you always know what you want to do next if you get interrupted, so you can build the right momentum much quicker. But beyond these two uses, microtasks may actually become a hindrance.

If you already know what to do and you are ready to jump straight into it, it's better just to jump straight into your work. If you are mentally prepared for the work ahead already and the urge to procrastinate is either manageable or non-existent, then there is no point to divert your attention from the task at hand. Just get it done while you are still mentally fresh and don't waste your mental energy on activities that, at this point, are unnecessary.

Diverting your attention from programming to splitting your work into microtasks is a form of context switching. And you already know that context switching wastes mental energy. If you have to choose between fighting the urge to procrastinate or splitting your work into microtasks, then the latter is indeed a better option. But if you already are able to get in gear and concentrate on your work, then having a mini planning session just uses up some mental energy that you would have otherwise spent doing the actual work.

Same applies to the situations when you have managed to enter the state of flow. You are already fully engaged in your work. You already know what to do next after you complete your current chunk of work. And all of this happens organically.

Yes, once you are no longer in the state of flow, it might be a good idea to have a planning session. But don't try to do it while you are still fully engaged in your work. If you have a planning session then, it might just take you out of "the zone" prematurely. It may break your flow. And, as a result, you will get less done than you would have otherwise. And the work that you manage to get done afterward might be of inferior quality.

To decide whether or not to use microtasks, there is a simple rule to follow. If, at any particular moment of time you know exactly what to do and there is sufficient enthusiasm to do it, then don't bother with microtasks. Otherwise, make it a habit to apply them.

You have now learned about one of the most effective tools for fighting procrastination, creating a momentum of productive work and entering the state of flow. But microtasks don't have to be the only tool in your arsenal. There are some other tools which are just as powerful, but are intended for some other purposes.

One of such tools is Shisa Kanko, which was originally developed in Japan, where it's heavily used in various industries, but is especially known for its applications in the railway industry.

Shisa Kanko was specifically designed to help its users to maintain a strong focus for long periods of time and prevent them from making any serious mistakes. Both of these benefits are very valuable in a programmer's job. And this system is universal enough to be applicable in any line of work, including programming.

This is why the next chapter has been dedicated to this system. You will learn what Shisa Kanko is and how you can benefit from it as a programmer.

References

1. Naomi Tutu - The Words of Desmond Tutu: Second Edition - William Morrow
2. Chris Northwood - The Full Stack Developer: Your Essential Guide to the Everyday Skills Expected of a Modern Full Stack Web Developer - Apress
3. Jocko Willink - Discipline Equals Freedom (Field Manual) - St. Martin's Press
4. Admiral William H. McRaven - Commencement Address - The University of Texas at Austin, May 17, 2014
5. Sam Neuman - Monolith to Microservices: Evolutionary Patterns to Transform Your Monolith – O'Reilly
6. Thomas Connolly - Database Systems: A Practical Approach to Design, Implementation, and Management, Global Edition - Pearson

CHAPTER 9

SHISA KANKO – A JAPANESE TECHNIQUE TO GET IN THE ZONE EASILY

It's important to externalise our activity, making it real and putting it into the world. When we take action out of our heads and embed action in the world, we suddenly have extra sources of information to help guide us. By embedding our behaviour in the world, we reduce the burden on memory, relying on new information about our tasks to guide ongoing action.

-- *Christopher Roosen*

People choose the programming profession for various reasons, which may include money and perceived prestige. But the people who succeed in the profession the most are usually the ones who had some degree of enthusiasm for technology in general or for programming in particular.

In popular culture, software development is often associated with something exciting. Software engineers are seen as inventors who build things that could only ever been previously seen in sci-fi movies. Although hardware engineers, designers and other tech professionals did their part too, all technological innovations that we take for granted in the modern world are powered by software.

It's software developers who enable us to instantly get in touch with each other and even see and hear each other in real time, even if we are located in different places of the world. It's software developers who have enabled cars to drive themselves. Without software developers, there would be no flying drones that can enable anyone to know what it feels like to be a pilot.

And those kinds of innovations are one of the biggest reasons why people choose to work as software developers. They want to be at the cutting edge of innovation. They want to participate in inventions of new products. And they see nothing but excitement in their future career.

But unfortunately, not everything you will do as a programmer will be flashy and exciting. Yes, if you choose the right niche and the right organization, then chances are that you will participate in a lot of exciting work. But even if you have ended up in the most innovative team within the most innovative technology niche, you will still have no choice but to regularly perform boring tasks.

You will have to write a lot of boilerplate code that is very similar to the code you've repeatedly written before. You'll have to write documentation. You'll have to write automated tests for your code to make sure that every part of it is working as expected. You will be fixing bugs in other people's code. And, among many other routine tasks, you will have to make sure software you write produces enough log entries and metrics to enable the tech support team (or even your own team) to diagnose problems with the software.

Mundane work is inevitable, even if it only occupies a part of your total volume of work. And this is the type of work where it's the hardest to maintain focus.

When the task that you do is boring, it will feel like a chore. Splitting it into microtasks will help somewhat, but it probably won't eliminate the feeling of boredom completely. In these situations, your mind will naturally be occupied with thoughts about things that are more exciting than the task you are currently doing. And those thoughts are the thing that will interfere with your focus.

When you can't give your task at hand 100% focus, there will be some issues. First of all, your task will take longer to complete compared to a task of a similar volume that you have managed to dedicate full focus on. You are also more likely to make a mistake.

Not being 100% focused may cause you to miss some critical detail. For the same reason, the quality of your output might not be as high as it could have been otherwise.

Also, when you aren't fully engaged, it's easy to lose track of what you've already done and what's left to do. In this disengaged state, it's easy to accidentally perform some duplicate work. And this will slow you down even further.

But the good news is that all of these problems are fixable. There is a Japanese technique known as *Shisa Kanko*, which was specifically designed to get you fully focused on a task that is mundane and repetitive. In Japan, it's routinely used in safety-critical industries, such as railway and manufacturing. And it has proven its effectiveness time and time again.

This technique helps you to fully immerse yourself in the work that you are doing, no matter how boring it is. Your productivity will increase, along with the quality of your output, while unintentional mistakes will become less likely.

When you are fully immersed in your work, the work will no longer seem boring. You will start deriving a degree of pleasure from it. And you will increase your chances of getting into the state of flow, even if the task at hand is not naturally conducive to it.

So first, let's find out what Shisa Kanko is, how it works and how it came about. Then, you will learn how to apply this technique in the context of software development.

How Shisa Kanko was developed to keep focus during boring tasks

If you have ever been at a train station in Japan or have seen one in a video, you might have noticed how various members of station staff are constantly making some hand gestures, while saying something to themselves. To an uninitiated eye, it may even look silly, especially if there is nobody else standing next to the person. [1] But this is precisely what Shisa Kanko is in action. And every member of the train station staff has been trained in it.

Shisa Kanko translates from Japanese as "Pointing and Calling". It's a technique where every mental action that you do is accompanied by a hand gesture and a verbal comment.

For example, when a train driver follows Shisa Kanko, he or she won't just look at the speedometer to check the train speed. The driver would point a finger at the speedometer and verbally describe what he or she is doing and announce what the current speed is.

Same applies to the railway track engineers whose job it is to walk around the tracks and check their condition. Instead of just looking in the direction of a specific section of a track and making a mental note that it is in a good condition, they would look at the track and verbally announce that it's in a good condition

Different types of railway staff make countless numbers of these routine checks throughout the day. The vast majority of those checks will just confirm that everything operates as normal. But when Shisa Kanko is applied, every single one of these checks is accompanied by hand gestures and verbal comments.

So, when you see what Japanese train station staff do, they don't just make a bunch of random movements and speak to themselves because they are so bored. On the contrary, they are following their protocols to the letter. And this protocol was specifically designed for them not to get bored and not miss any crucial details.

Shisa Kanko isn't just a bunch of pointless rituals that are performed because Japanese railway bosses wanted their staff to do them. The reason why this system has been universally applied in the railway industry in Japan for a very long time, and then got adopted by other industries and other countries, is because it has proven its effectiveness in terms of safety and performance.

The Japanese railway is known across the world for its excellent punctuality and safety. Even the high-speed trains are rarely delayed by more than one minute, and that's despite the fact that Japan is a densely populated country with a complex infrastructure. [2] Of course, it was made possible by excellent planning. But in part, this has been achieved by the fact that everyone involved in the operation of the railway network is fully focused at all times. This allows them to spot problems quickly and deal with them in a timely manner. Force majeure situations, which are inevitable on a railway network, especially if it's as complex as the one in Japan, are dealt with while they are still easily manageable. And it's Shisa Kanko that ensures that every member of the railway staff remains fully focused while they are on their shift

But why is Shisa Kanko so effective at helping people to maintain their focus? And is there any scientific evidence that confirms its effectiveness? Well, it turns out that it's the simplicity of the technique that makes it so effective. And its effectiveness is indeed supported by plenty of scientific evidence.

What makes Shisa Kanko so effective?

So, where did the system of Shisa Kanko originate from? Well, it happens that its origins are difficult to trace, but many attribute it to Yasoichi Hori, who worked as a train engineer at the beginning of the 20th century. His eyesight was gradually failing, so, to minimize the chance of making a mistake, he started to verbally call out signals that he saw, which were then confirmed by his fireman.

It's hard to tell whether this was indeed the first use of Shisa Kanko in practice. But the behavior made it into the official railway operation manual in 1913. [3]

Even though the technique of pointing and calling has probably originated in a non-scientific environment, its effectiveness has since been repeatedly validated by science. For example, a group of researchers from the Railway Technical Research Institute of Japan found that pointing and calling reduces human errors by almost 85% when applied to simple, mundane and repetitive tasks where some degree of decision making is involved. The baseline error rate was roughly 2.38 per 100 tasks. This went down to approximately 0.38 when pointing and calling was implemented. [4]

But it's not just the reduction of human errors where Shisa Kanko has been scientifically proven to be very effective. Research has also shown that it increases performance both during repetitive tasks and during tasks switching.

A multi-disciplinary team of researchers conducted an experiment where they have asked participants to perform a series of tasks. Depending on the test group, the rules of these tasks would either keep changing or stay the same. Also, depending on the group, the participants would be asked to either point and call during their tasks or not to.

The results clearly showed that pointing and calling does indeed improve the performance. This is as true for repetitive tasks with unchanging rules as it is for tasks where the rules keep changing. Pointing and calling doesn't only help you to maintain your focus while you are doing something mundane and repetitive. It happens to also help you to switch tasks more effectively. And, despite all the additional actions of gesturing and talking, the participants reported that pointing and calling didn't increased cognitive load. [5]

The reason why Shisa Kanko is so effective is because coordinating multiple body systems to achieve a particular task kicks you out of the autopilot mode. And it also leaves very little room for any thoughts that would interfere with the task at hand.

This is why Shisa Kanko is a universal tool for helping you to maintain focus in any situation involving mundane and repeated work. Although the technique has originated in the railway industry, its usefulness is not specific to any industry.

Why Shisa Kanko is not just for railways

Stuart Kay, a director of Cambridge Medtech Solutions, a company that specializes in design and development of medical devices, is a big proponent of Shisa Kanko. He has extensively researched the system and has been actively promoting its use in the medical field as one of the most effective tools of minimizing human errors. He highlighted the following reasons behind its effectiveness:

> *"Shisa Kanko is a behaviour based approach using auditory, kinesthetic and visual stimuli to prevent tasks being carried out with a lack of attention. Instead of functioning on 'autopilot' to carry out routine tasks, the individual performs a coordinated response requiring him/her to point at the object of*

> *the action and call out its status. The process requires focus and attention and reduces the probability of user error.*
>
> *Scientific research reveals an increase in blood flow to the frontal lobe of the brain when an individual uses Shisa Kanko; the frontal lobe is an area of the brain that controls attention. Shisa Kanko sharpens focus and attention while reinforcing learning and strengthening neural pathways. Incidence of error is drastically reduced, the potential is great."* [6]

Christopher Roosed, a UX designer and a blogger, is another big proponent of Shisa Kanko. He said the following about the technique:

> *"It's important to externalise our activity, making it real and putting it into the world. When we take action out of our heads and embed action in the world, we suddenly have extra sources of information to help guide us. By embedding our behaviour in the world, we reduce the burden on memory, relying on new information about our tasks to guide ongoing action."*

The universal effectiveness of Shisa Kanko across any industry is the reason why it's often promoted within the context of various corporate and industrial performance-enhancement systems, such as Lean Six Sigma. [7]

In software development, safety isn't as important as it is in the railway industry or medicine, unless it's some critical infrastructure components that are being developed. But even so, software development mistakes can cost you dearly. And, as a programmer, you will have to keep an eye on your performance and the quality of your output. This is why Shisa Kanko is applicable in the software development industry.

And now we will have a look at how you, as a programmer, can take advantage of this system.

How to apply Shisa Kanko in the context of programming

As a programmer, you aren't just standing on the platform and looking at things. You are already doing quite a lot of typing, even when what you are typing is just some boilerplate code that you've typed countless times before. So, is there any room left for pointing and calling, if your hands are already occupied? Well, as it turns out, there is.

A train driver would also need to operate various controls with their hands. But despite this, as we already know, Shisa Kanko isn't just something that doesn't interfere with their activities, but makes them more effective.

Calling

When you are doing something that is necessary but isn't particularly exciting, a good place to start would be to start verbalizing what you are doing. So, don't just write boilerplate code in silence. And don't put your headphones on during the process to listen to something in the background, because the task at hand is so unbearably boring. Instead, write the code and narrate every step of it.

Instead of just typing your code in, type it while saying something along the lines of "I am writing a function (insert name), which is needed for (insert purpose)". Or you can use something even more fine-grained and literally narrate everything that you type. This would be something like "I am opening the code block with a curly bracket. I am now declaring a variable (insert name), which will hold the value of (insert value), which is (insert the name of the data type)".

You may need to apply some trial and error to determine the way of narrating your actions that works best for you. It doesn't even have to be done in a specific prescribed way. Verbalizing anything that's directly related to what you are currently doing will help you to immerse yourself in your work.

And if you are writing documentation rather than code, you can use exactly the same principles too. Instead of just typing your text in, you can also say it out loud. This way, you'll obtain stronger focus

214

and your work won't be half-hearted, regardless of how mundane this documentation is.

Using verbalizations can be effective not only while you are already working on a task, but before you even start. Saying out loud what the structure of your code or your document should be before you start writing it would help you to determine if there aren't any nuances that you haven't considered or any details you have missed. It will help you to affirm to yourself that your planned action is good enough and, if you find that it is not, it will help you determine how to make the action better.

Even if you get completely stuck and you don't know what your next action should be, as sometimes happens in programming, you will still find that verbalizations are useful. In this case, you can just start thinking out loud. And this is what will maintain your focus, so you will eventually come up with the right plan. Otherwise, you might just get overwhelmed by distracting thoughts and give in to procrastination.

Don't worry about looking silly while you are narrating your actions while you are working in a busy office. There are ways you can modify this practice to make it invisible to your colleagues. We will cover those in a later section.

Verbalization is just one half of Shisa Kanko. The other half of it is pointing, which is just as important. And it has its own utility in programming.

Pointing

Of course, you can't point while you are typing. Making regular pauses while you are typing to point at something will be counterproductive. Not only will it make you longer to complete the task, but you may also experience a heavier cognitive load due to context switching. But almost any activity that doesn't involve typing can be enhanced by pointing.

Pointing at the screen while reading complex code helps you to keep track of where you are. When you have a soup of keywords, variable names, semicolons and curly braces on the screen, it's sometimes easy to get lost in it. But when you point at a specific place that you are interested in, all irrelevant content gets filtered out of your mind.

But pointing is not only helpful to ensure that you don't get lost in the code. After all, the workers of the railway industry, where the practice originated, don't use it for this purpose. Pointing is just another anchor to embed you in the process even more.

So, when you are about to write some code and you are saying out loud what this code will be while pointing your finger at the place where this code will go–at the same time, sending an increased blood flow to your attention-controlling frontal lobe–that particular bit of code will be the only thing on your mind at that moment.

Now, we will get back to one major obstacle that you, as a developer, may encounter while trying to implement Shisa Kanko in practice. It's easy to do pointing and calling while you cannot be seen or heard by anyone, but what about the office environment? After all, talking to yourself while pointing your fingers at the screen is not a behavior that's typical for the office

Well, there are ways of dealing with this. Let's talk about them next.

How to avoid feeling embarrassed using Shisa Kanko in the office

The idea of using Shisa Kanko in the context of software development is not new. Like some other techniques that have originated in other industries, such as lean manufacturing, it has already been tried and tested by various companies in the Silicon Valley. And this is a good thing, because those examples can be cited to persuade your whole team to adopt this practice.

This is the best way to practice Shisa Kanko in the office while avoiding embarrassment. You cannot get embarrassed if what you do becomes normal in the context that you do it in. Nobody will view your pointing and calling behavior odd if everyone else in your team is doing it too.

If your entire team is onboard with Shisa Kanko practice, you can even turn it into something that is really fun to do. Scott Vandehey, a senior front-end developer and a blogger, described a way of turning Shisa Kanko into a fun team activity. But to do so, it has been slightly modified. Instead of pointing and calling, it turns into "pointing and shouting".

This is what Scott Vandehey suggested:

> *"Enter the "Point and Shout" method. (We're Americans, shouting was the natural next step in the process.) Now, instead of writing code quietly and posting in the company Slack channel requesting a code review, a developer must coordinate their attention with physical and verbal confirmations to ensure they're following the process. Imagine the following:*
>
> *Alice has written some code. When she's ready to put her code up for review, before she hits the button to post it, she points to her passing tests in a terminal window and calls out "TESTS PASSING!" Then she points to her well-written commit message and calls out "INFORMATIVE COMMIT MESSAGE WRITTEN!" Finally, she points to the button and calls out "PUSHING CODE FOR REVIEW!"*
>
> *Bob hears all this (how could he not, he sits right next to Alice!), and opens her code review. He pulls her branch, tests the change in the browser, verifies the tests are passing and reads her code. He sees some changes she should make and leaves a helpful comment. Before submitting, he points to his well-written and informative comments and calls out "POSTING FEEDBACK TO ALICE'S CODE REVIEW!""*
> [9]

This practice has an added bonus in companies where developers want to work remotely, while company bosses want everyone to work on site. If the company happens to be based in an open space office, then there is nothing that would work better than this constant shouting from the developer's team corner to persuade the bosses to let the developers work remotely.

Of course, this example was meant to be a joke. But jokes aside, adopting Shisa Kanko as a standard technique practiced by the team is the best way to avoid the embarrassment while practicing it. Also, constantly hearing somebody else narrating their actions out loud will remind you to do it yourself. The team will provide the echo chamber effect that we have discussed in chapter 4.

But what if your team is not onboard with this practice? Or what if you are too embarrassed to even suggest it to the team? Well, if you can't get your team to adopt Shisa Kanko, then you can still practice it on your own and avoid embarrassment while doing so.

How to practice Shisa Kanko when nobody else will

If nobody else around you is doing routine pointing and calling, then there is a limit to how much you can practice it and avoid the embarrassment. But fortunately, you can modify the procedure to make it more subtle.

The action of pointing is probably not even a problem to start with. If you imagine an office worker pointing at their screen while being focused on a task, you will probably see that this action wouldn't look very odd at all.

Pointing is what we routinely do, especially when we are focused on what we are doing. It's normal to see a person pointing at the text while reading a book. And it's normal to see someone occasionally pointing at the screen.

If you aren't comfortable with pointing, imagine what it looks like to an external observer: like you're just concentrating. And then, practice it. Being comfortable while performing this action is just like any other habit you can build.

You can recall from chapter 1 how neural pathways in our brain are formed. Neural pathways don't only control habitual actions, but also create mental associations. And they get reinforced by repeated practice.

So, if you start regularly pointing at the screen while performing mundane repetitive tasks, you will eventually start to automatically do it while performing these types of tasks. But also, if you won't be receiving any criticism from anyone for doing this action (which you almost definitely won't), your brain will dissociate this action from embarrassment. You will get comfortable with it.

The "calling" part of pointing and calling practice is a different story though. Talking to yourself out loud will feel embarrassing.

Of course, you can just explain to your colleagues what you are doing and get out of your comfort zone. If you are the only one in the office who habitually narrates their actions, you may gain supreme confidence. And maybe you'll eventually get the rest of your team on board with it. But you don't actually have to venture that far out of your comfort zone to make the practice of narrating your actions useful.

Even if you narrate your actions in a barely noticeable whisper that only you can hear, you will still be taking advantage of the practice. It will still help you to anchor yourself in the present moment and leave no room for distracting thoughts.

And someone moving their lips while focusing on a task won't look odd in an office environment, just like someone who's pointing at the screen. On the contrary, such a person would look fully engaged.

So, the same thing applies here as it does with pointing. If you initially feel embarrassed about making inaudible narration of your actions, you can imagine that to your colleagues you just look fully engaged and practice it more.

You can make it even easier for yourself. Instead of even moving your lips, you can just make a mental announcement in your head when you have completed an action. However, this is probably the least effective way of helping you to gain focus. After all, it's just a thought. And even though deliberately thinking this thought makes less room for some distracting thoughts, it doesn't fully immerse you in the current task. It doesn't engage your vocal system. Therefore, only do this if making quiet whispers still feels unbearably embarrassing to you. Otherwise, use your mouth to announce your actions, even if it's in a way that nobody can hear them.

Once you get comfortable with practicing Shisa Kanko, it will pay you off in more than one way. Not only will you be able to maintain your focus during the most boring tasks, but you may also be able to get into the state of flow, even though mundane repetitive tasks aren't by themselves conducive to it.

How Shisa Kanko will get you in the flow during the most boring tasks

In chapter 2, we have discussed what is the state of flow and how to get into it. And it appears that the types of tasks that are the least conducive to the state of flow are the ones that are way too difficult or the ones that are way too easy. Mundane and repetitive tasks fall under the latter category.

The tasks that are the most conducive to the state of flow are the ones that are neither too difficult nor too easy. They are easy enough that you feel that you are making progress. But they are not so easy that you feel bored and disengaged. As long as you can prevent yourself from getting disengaged, you can still enter the state of flow even with easy routine tasks. And Shisa Kanko has been precisely designed to prevent you from getting disengaged.

Let's recall what characteristics define the state of flow. As you may recall from the chapter 2, they are the following:

- Concentration that is intensely focused on the present moment

- Action and awareness are perceived to be one

- Sense of self disappears

- A strong sense of control over the present situation

- Distorted perception of time

- Sense of pleasure from the activity being performed

If any of these are missing, then you aren't really in the state of flow. But Shisa Kanko happens to be good at bringing about these. Let's see how.

- **Concentration that is intensely focused on the present moment.** The main purpose of Shisa Kanko is to anchor you in the present moment and get you to focus on the activity you are currently performing. The pointing and calling ritual is done to synchronize as many of your body as possible with the task at hand. And that leaves little to no room for something that can interfere with your focus.

- **Action and awareness are perceived to be one.** When you are performing Shisa Kanko, you are thinking about the action while forcing yourself to not to think about anything else. This may get you immersed in your action to such an extent that it occupies your whole awareness. You may temporarily lose awareness of anything else. Your awareness will become one with your action.

- **Sense of self disappears.** When you are performing some mental action, while also pointing at the physical subject of your thoughts and announcing your actions with your vocal system, you may get immersed into your action to such an extent that you won't perceive anything else outside of it. If your physical body and your thoughts are dedicated to a specific activity, you may even lose the perception of self. There will be no separate "you". You and the activity will become one.

- **A strong sense of control over the present situation.** One of the reasons that Shisa Kanko became so widely adopted by safety-critical industries is to make sure that personnel have full control over the processes at all times. And this works well, as we already had a look at how Shisa Kanko improves the performance and reduces accidents.

  When you are fully embedded in the present moment, you will naturally have a sense of control over the situation.

- **Distorted perception of time.** When you force yourself to get embedded in the current tasks, quite naturally, you won't be looking at the clock. And neither will you be thinking about the duration of your activity.

When you aren't thinking of time, then the sense of time may get distorted. When you are feeling engaged, it becomes easy to lose track of time.

- **Sense of pleasure from the activity being performed.** Can you imagine being fully engaged in an activity and not feel some degree of pleasure? It's unlikely to be the case.

  When you don't enjoy something, you can't get fully engaged in it. Instead of being engaged, you will just be thinking about the unpleasantness of the activity.

  Being fully immersed in an activity you don't like is an example of cognitive dissonance. And the brain doesn't like the feeling of cognitive dissonance. So it will tell us that we are enjoying the activity we've managed to fully focus on, even if the activity isn't intrinsically pleasant.

  Boring and repetitive tasks are inherently unpleasant. And the reason why Shisa Kanko is so effective at making you engaged during these tasks is because it removes the sense of displeasure. And it has been found to improve the overall feeling of job satisfaction. [10]

So, as you can see, by its design, Shisa Kanko can indeed help you to enter the state of flow even during tasks that aren't normally compatible with this highly productive mental state.

State of flow occurs when you manage to get yourself fully immersed in an activity. And if an activity is exciting enough, then this immersion will occur naturally. But if the activity is unbearably boring, you have to use external tools to make it immersive, like Shisa Kanko. But once you have managed to get yourself fully engaged, it doesn't matter how mundane the original task was. You may be able to enter the state of flow regardless.

And there are ways of making your Shisa Kanko practice even more effective. Just like any activity, the more you do it–the better at it you become. And the more effective the practice becomes in its application.

Make Shisa Kanko a habit and never feel bored in your job again

The first time you try Shisa Kanko, it may feel uncomfortable. In fact, it may even feel ineffective, as you may be thinking about whether or not you are performing the method properly instead of focusing on your task. But over time, it will start getting more and more natural.

The risk of Shisa Kanko distracting you from your action rather than helping you focus on it is very low. The reason why Shisa Kanko consists of such simple rituals is precisely so it doesn't create another mental barrier that would make the task even harder to do. But nevertheless, any unfamiliar activity, including Shisa Kanko, may not be as effective as it should be the first time you use it.

But continued practice will reap rewards. As we have already discussed in chapter 1, neural pathways that get built in the brain during habit formation aren't only responsible for a physical action of the body. They are responsible for mental associations too.

When you manage to successfully apply Shisa Kanko to get yourself fully focused on the task at hand enough times, the ritual becomes something more than just a tool to get you to focus. It becomes something akin to Pavlov's dog's bell.

Your brain starts associating pointing and calling with mental focus. So, the mere presence of these actions may trigger the focused state of mind in you. You won't even have to wait for these actions to have their intended effect.

Also, if you apply Shisa Kanko enough times while dealing with routine activities, you will no longer have to consciously think about doing pointing and calling while performing those activities. Those activities will become a natural trigger for Shisa Kanko. With practice, it will become a self-reinforcing virtual cycle.

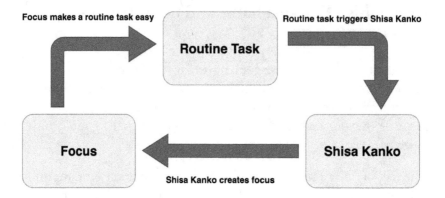

Routine task triggers Shisa Kanko. Shisa Kanko triggers the state of mental focus. Mental focus makes it easier to complete the routine task. And it all continues until you no longer have any routine tasks left on your list.

The benefits of Shisa Kanko don't stop here. After you get comfortable performing the ritual in your work, you can try it out in your everyday life.

Shisa Kanko is useful way beyond software development

Have you ever had a nagging thought that you may not have locked your door after leaving the house? Or were you ever worried that you might have forgotten to switch off the cooker?

Well, we've all been there. When we do routine things, we tend to do them on autopilot. And when things are done on autopilot, the brain doesn't give the task a lot of its resources in the form of attention.

And we aren't really good at remembering anything that we do on autopilot. This is why you don't always remember whether or not you have locked your front door. But with Shisa Kanko, you can make this forgetfulness a thing of the past.

Pointing and calling forces you into the present moment. When you perform it, you are no longer doing things on autopilot. And this way, you will distinctly remember that you have closed the door.

If it's not only the habitual wrist movement that turns your key, but it's also accompanied by a verbal announcement and additional hand gesture, then chances are that the action will get embedded in your memory.

This checklist-like nature of Shisa Kanko is equally as appropriate in any other situation where checklists are applicable. Checklists are designed to transfer a completed activity from your head to either a piece of paper or a digital device. With them, you won't even have to remember the activity. It's perfectly fine to do it on autopilot. The tick on the checklist can always confirm that the activity has been done.

But the checklists are not always practical or a medium to do one on isn't always available. And this is where Shisa Kanko can act as a checklist directly embedded in your memory. Instead of having your action written down, you can make yourself easily remember that you have completed it.

And that is something that is useful for non-technical aspects of your work too. For example, this is how Shisa Kanko will ensure that you are fully prepared for an important meeting. Or, if you are fully prepared, it will eliminate the nagging feeling that you may have forgotten something.

But Shisa Kanko is far from being the only technique that will help you to maintain focus during boring routine work. Likewise, microtasks aren't the only technique that will help you to deal with large chunks of work. There are also some time management tricks that will help you during both of these types of work.

In the next chapter, we will have a look at some of these techniques. You will learn how to use timers to aggressively separate your day into chunks of productive periods.

We will cover one of the most popular time management tricks–the Pomodoro technique. But you will also learn why Pomodoro is not a panacea that will be equally effective for everyone. You will learn how to come up with the most effective use of timers for you personally.

But time management tricks like Pomodoro go well beyond just helping you to maintain focus and trick your brain to work when it feels like procrastinating. These tricks will help you to squeeze the most out of the limited time that's available to you.

Time is a very precious non-renewable resource. So let's learn how to use it wisely.

References

1. Atlas Obscura (2020) What's the Point of Pointing in Japan, Anyway? - https://www.youtube.com/watch?v=RZun7IvqMvE
2. N. Tomii - How the punctuality of the Shinkansen has been achieved - Chiba Institute of Technology, Japan
3. Alice Gordenker - JR gestures - The Japan Times, 21 October, 2008 - https://www.japantimes.co.jp/news/2008/10/21/reference/jr-gestures
4. Masayoshi Shigemori, Ayanori Sato, Takayuki Masuda - Experience-based PC learning system for for human error prevention by point-and-call checks - Railway Technical Research Institute - QR or RTRI, Vol. 53, No 4, November 2012
5. Kazumitsu Shinohara, Hiroshi Naito, Yuko Matsui and Masaru Hikono - The effects of "finger pointing and calling" on cognitive control processes in the task-switching paradigm - International Journal of Industrial Ergonomics, Volume 43, Issue 2, March 2013, Pages 129-136
6. Stuart Kay - Shisa Kanko could reduce mistakes and save lives - LinkedIn Pulse - https://www.linkedin.com/pulse/shisa-kanko-could-reduce-mistakes-save-lives-stuart-kay/
7. Christopher Roosen - How The Ritual of Pointing and Calling - Shisa Kanko - Embeds Us In The World - Adventures in a design world, April 2020 - https://www.christopherroosen.com/blog/2020/4/20/how-the-ritual-of-pointing-and-calling-shisa-kanko-embeds-us-in-the-world
8. Shisa Kanko - Glossary, Lean Six Sigma Definition - https://www.leansixsigmadefinition.com/glossary/shisa-kanko/
9. Scott Vandehey - Pointing and Shouting Your Way to Better Code - https://spaceninja.com/2017/04/01/pointing-and-shouting-your-way-to-better-code/

10. Jonathan Shurlock, James Rudd, Annette Jeanes, Aphrodite Iacovidou, Antonio Creta, Vijayabharathy Kanthasamy, Richard Schilling, Eamonn Sullivan, Joanne Cooke, Colette Laws-Chapman, David Baxter and Malcolm Finlay - Communication in the intensive care unit during COVID-19: early experience with the Nightingale Communication Method - International Journal for Quality in Health Care, Volume 33, Issue 1, 2021

CHAPTER 10

MAKING WORK EASY WITH POMODORO AND TIMERS

One day we will be more creative, more productive and yet more relaxed. Unleash Innovation!

-- *Francesco Cirillo*

You'll have gathered by now that a good portion of this book is about reprogramming our thoughts and behaviors. But in the last two chapters we've taken a slightly different approach and started tricking our brains. Let's do more of that in this final chapter on making work easy, before we bring all we've learned together.

As we have covered in chapter 8, the best way to keep your productivity up while dealing with large tasks is to split it into small atomic microtasks. This way, your brain will think that the work ahead is much smaller than it actually is, so you will find it easier to dedicate your full focus to those activities.

In chapter 9, you learned how to use the Japanese technique of Shisa Kanko to keep yourself fully engaged even during the most boring tasks. Using your voice to announce your actions, while pointing at your code, leaves little room in your head for any distracting thoughts and anchors you in the moment. This way, your work will feel less boring, you are more likely to complete it faster and you are much less likely to make any mistakes.

But there is another effective technique that you can use to trick your brain to not get overwhelmed by large tasks, not get distracted while doing boring tasks, and maintain your focus easily. And this technique involves strategic use of timers.

There are variations of this technique, the most popular of which is known as Pomodoro. We will cover this technique and specific variations to suit you in this chapter, but the fundamental principles are the same, regardless of which method you choose to use. You can use it in conjunction with microtasks and Shisa Kanko, but it's also effective on its own.

Using timers involves splitting your day into pre-defined periods of work and rest. While you are in a work period, you maintain full focus on the task at hand. And then, once the period is up and you hear the bell ringing, you have to force yourself to stop and have a break.

The technique splits seemingly large tasks into small chunks, so it is effective at tricking your brain to see your work as much more manageable. But, on top of that, being aware of the timer creates a sense of urgency, so you become more motivated to work and it becomes easier to maintain focus.

Perhaps you have been in a situation where you procrastinated in your task right until only a couple of hours were left before the deadline. But then, once the realization of the imminent deadline has kicked in, you could just put yourself together and do all the remaining work in a few hours without even taking a break. And there is a similar mechanism at play when you are working against an artificial deadline of a timer.

We will have a detailed look at how the idea of using timers as a productivity hack came about and why this technique is so effective. But first, we will address one apparent contradiction that you may have noticed.

In chapter 2, we have talked about the importance of deep work and why you need large chunks of interrupted time to achieve it. Also, when talking about the state of flow, we have covered how it takes time (normally at least 15 minutes) to ease yourself into this productive mental state. If you then get interrupted, it will take you the same amount of time to achieve the state of flow, assuming you manage to achieve it at all.

So, you may want to ask the question of whether using timers artificially creates such interruptions when none are needed and prevents you from ever entering the state of flow. Well, the answer to this is both yes and no.

Yes, timers may become the enemy of deep work during the tasks that would normally benefit from prolonged periods of intense focus. But these types of challenging work that require you to have an uninterrupted deep thinking session are relatively rare, even in intellectually demanding professions like programming. We will cover specific cases where using timers may be a hindrance rather than an enhancement.

But during most tasks that programmers do, it's not strictly necessary to maintain prolonged uninterrupted focus. Splitting your work into a number of short sessions of relatively deep focus will suffice.

Let's have a look at some reasons why prolonged deep work may not always be achievable.

Why you can't always do prolonged deep work

Well, the key reason why prolonged deep work is not always achievable is because such an activity uses a lot of mental resources that our brain is so desperately trying to preserve. As we have discussed in chapter 2, unless you have managed to enter the state of flow, there will still be some part of your attention that isn't strictly focused on the task at hand. And this split between trying to maintain intense focus and being mindful of other things is what drains your mental energy.

If you don't manage to get into the state of flow, then having breaks will actually help you with the activities that require deep focus rather than hinder them. Do you remember how, in chapter 2, we used a metaphor with hypothetical units of energy to explain why doing deep work while not maintaining 100% focus will make you drain your mental resources to the state where maintaining focus will be all but impossible? Well, in this case, forcing yourself to take breaks would be the only way to restore your energy and, with it, restore your ability to maintain focus.

But there is more to it. In chapter 9, we already discussed that a lot of activities that programmers engage in are just routine tasks that don't require a very focused engagement. These activities consist of writing some standard boilerplate code, writing unit tests, writing documentation, reading somebody else's code, etc.

It's still important to maintain your focus during mundane repetitive tasks, as can be achieved with Shisa Kanko. But you don't really have to dedicate a prolonged uninterrupted work session to complete these tasks. In fact, this is where the opposite might be better.

There is a concept known as Parkinson's Law, which explains how applying more resources to a job doesn't necessarily make the process of completing that job more efficient. To paraphrase it and make it sound simpler, we can describe this principle as follows:

> *"The amount of work will always expand to fill any additional time it has been given."* [1]

Cyril Northcote Parkinson came up with this principle while he was working as a civil servant. He noticed that hiring more people didn't make government departments work faster. On the contrary, the departments were growing bigger, while the amount of the useful output they produced was remaining the same or even shrinking in size. For example, when the British government body that used to oversee the administration of colonies was renamed to The Foreign Office it had the highest number of employees it ever had, despite having no colonies to administer. [2]

How exactly Parkinson's Law works is beyond the scope of our discussion. But what's important to know is that it's as applicable to the work done by individuals as it is to the work done by government departments.

To apply it in the context of doing mundane and repetitive programming tasks, you probably won't manage to make yourself more efficient by giving yourself longer sessions to work on them, all the while attempting to focus. Instead, you will probably just end up doing more of them, some of which wouldn't even have been necessary. Or you may drag those tasks out and spend more time that you would otherwise have on each of the tasks. Even if you maintain full focus during your work, you won't really gain any additional benefit from spending more time on a task, if the task in question is nothing but a routine activity.

Why keeping focused sometimes needs to be a sprint rather than a marathon

After reading chapter 9, you know why Shisa Kanko is so effective at keeping you focused during mundane work. But it's also good when you can complete that mundane work as quickly as possible and get it out of the way, so you can finally do something more enjoyable.

Yes, when Shisa Kanko was developed in the railway industry in Japan, getting things done quickly wasn't an emphasis of it. Trains arrive and depart on schedule, so your job as a railway worker is to ensure that certain activities get performed on schedule.

But software development doesn't operate on schedule. There are deadlines looming. And, for a programmer, the goal of a typical working day would be to complete as much as possible within the constraints of available time and not make any mistakes while doing so.

Of course, if you strive to be a good developer that everyone would want to hire, it is also important that your work stands out. You can't afford to merely solve a problem. Your solution must be of a high quality, so people would prefer it over any alternatives.

But this principle only applies when you are engaged in creative parts of your job, such as architectural design, user interface styling, looking for opportunities to improve the amount of code covered by automated tests, etc. During those activities, you can always find ways to improve. So, it is important that you don't rush through these activities.

But mundane routine tasks, on the other hand, don't normally fall into this category. With those, the outcomes are usually well-known and binary. Either the task is completed or it is not. And the task was either completed without errors or with them. That's it. There is no further room to improve the outcomes of such a task. Attempting to do so would be a waste of time. All you have to do is spend some time typing something in to achieve this outcome.

Boilerplate code will have some standard predefined structure. Your job will just be to type this structure up. Documentation that is intended for internal consumption is not a novel. As long as it sufficiently explains what the system does, it's good enough. A unit test would be nothing more than a block of code that verifies if a function would give the correct output if a specific input was passed into it.

Therefore, if you are working on a mundane routine activity, your goal is to complete it as quickly as possible and not make any mistakes while doing so. And it's better for your personal wellbeing if you can get as many of these tasks out of the way as possible and have a break, rather than fill the same amount of time without leaving any room for breaks. And this is the goal that timers are well suited to help you with.

As we shall see, splitting your working day into timed chunks of work has many advantages. But the most obvious advantage of using timers comes from the fact that, just like microtasks, they make it easier for you to defeat the desire to procrastinate.

How applying timers will help you to avoid procrastination

Just like microtasks, timers would split your work into smaller chunks. But instead of splitting it into atomic objectives, you would split it into time-based chunks.

But to your brain that wants to preserve its energy, the effect is broadly the same. When you know that you need to carry on working for only a relatively small period of time until the bell rings, it becomes easy to convince yourself not to procrastinate. But instead of saying to yourself that it's just a small piece of functionality that needs to be added before you can take a break, you tell yourself that you just need to focus for a short period of time and then you can have as much rest as you need.

How exactly you organize the timers will be up to you. No two people are the same and what works for me won't necessarily work for you. You can just assign several timed rounds of work that run back-to-back until you feel like you want to have a break. Or you can use something like Pomodoro, where you force yourself to take a short break after every round of work.

But timers aren't just effective at keeping yourself free of distractions. They will also help you to complete more work in less time. And this is especially true for mundane routine tasks. And this is because of how our brains perceive deadlines.

When you set a timer, you are, essentially, creating a deadline for yourself. It's not a concrete deadline. You aren't expected to achieve a specific goal before it. But it's a deadline nonetheless, and when we have an awareness of an imminent deadline, we become motivated by it: Your goal becomes to get as much work done as possible until the deadline lapses. Focus comes naturally to us. And it takes less effort to achieve good efficiency. [3]

Of course, deadlines can be stressful. This is especially true when you realize that you may not be able to accomplish everything you wanted to accomplish on time. But the artificial deadlines that we create for ourselves by implementing timers are not of this kind: They're flexible and are somewhat arbitrary.

Essentially, if you have told yourself that a specific period of time will be dedicated only to productive activities and nothing else, and if you know that this period will end soon, it will be easy for you to work non-stop until the bell rings. It will also be easier to not make any unnecessary pauses or let yourself get distracted.

When you know that shortly you will be able to legitimately make a pause or spend a couple of minutes browsing the web, it becomes much easier not to engage in these activities while you are doing something productive. And this is how timers can help you to close as many mundane tasks as possible as quickly as possible. You will be able to keep crunching them one after another until the bell rings.

And, just like any other habits, the habit of using timers will get better with practice. The timer will be embedded in your neural pathways as a string association with productive work. Eventually, a mere ring of the bell may trigger the right mental state for productive work. And you won't even be thinking about anything else.

But once the bell rings and the timer stops, there are a number of things you can do next. You stop and take as long as you need for a break. Or you may start another round and just carry on doing these rounds until you are legitimately tired. But one of the best ways of using such timers that has proven its effectiveness is the Pomodoro Technique. And this is what we will talk about next.

Where the Pomodoro Technique came from

The Pomodoro Technique is perhaps the best-known way of using timers to force yourself into periods of focused concentration. It was invented by Francesco Cirillo in the 1980s when he was still a university student. This technique has brought him fame, as many people found it to be effective. This helped him to have a successful career in the IT industry as the coach of Agile methodology.

"Pomodoro" is the Italian word for "tomato". And the idea of it is based on a tomato-shaped kitchen timer.

The technique is fairly simple. You set a timer for 25 minutes. During this time, you focus on your work. But once the bell rings, you force yourself to stop and take a break for 5 minutes. Then, you repeat the process. [4]

One round of work is known as one Pomodoro. After performing three or four Pomodoros, you take a longer break of 15 to 30 minutes. And you repeat the cycle until your working day is over.

Francesco Cirillo said the following about the Pomodoro technique that he invented:

> *"I discovered that you could learn how to improve your effectiveness and be better able to estimate how long a task will take to complete by recording how you utilize your time." [4]*

This quote emphasizes another important feature of the Pomodoro Technique. When you have been doing it for a while, you will get better at estimating the size of the task ahead of you. You will have trained yourself to see each task as requiring a particular number of Pomodoros.

Overall, The Pomodoro Technique has six objectives, which are the following: [5]

- **Find out how much effort an activity requires.** When you perform the Pomodoro Technique, you would have a ToDo list and you would record how many Pomodoros you would spend on each task. And this is what allows you to better estimate the size of similar tasks in the future.

- **Cut down on interruptions.** With the Pomodoro Technique, you plan your interruptions in, so you don't get spontaneously distracted during your productive activities. And this allows you to minimize the amount of interruptions you have.

  Also, your productive rounds are designed to be short enough for most people to be able to maintain focus. On the other hand, when you don't have such a strict time limit for a productive activity, you may get interrupted spontaneously and it may get out of your control.

- **Estimate the effort for activities.** This ties up to the first goal. Once you are used to the technique, you will be able to relatively accurately estimate the effort for any activities you are about to start.

- **Make Pomodoro more effective.** When you have been doing Pomodoro for a while, you will be able to adjust your activities around the technique for maximum effectiveness. For example, after having a break, you may spend the first few minutes of a new Pomodoro round to review what you have done in the previous round.

- **Define your own objectives.** The Pomodoro Technique allows you to re-evaluate and refine your objectives. For example, you may find that you have been spending too much time on a particular activity, while neglecting some other important activity.

Why Pomodoro is considered to be the best technique of timed work

But why is the Pomodoro Technique structured the way it is? Why does it consist of 25 minute chunks of work? What is it actually based on?

Well, the duration of productive rounds in the Pomodoro Technique is determined by two factors. Firstly, those periods are short enough, so your brain perceives them as very manageable chunks of work. Secondly, it's the amount of time that you can delay replying to a work-related email without experiencing any negative consequences. [5]

When you are performing a Pomodoro, you are focusing on purely productive activities. Routine tasks, like replying to emails, are not part of it. If those need to be done, it's the time between the Pomodoros that you fit those activities into.

As a programmer, you will receive emails and chat messages from time to time that need to be addressed urgently. So, dedicating just a specific part of the day to check your emails will not be applicable to most situations. But it's unlikely that you will be expected to reply to those the very minute you receive it, so you will still probably be able to afford a delay of up to 25 minutes.

Pomodoro Technique is simple. But its simplicity is precisely what made it take the world of IT by a storm. What makes this technique so good is that people who have tried it have experienced benefits beyond what they originally expected.

The benefits of using Pomodoro timers

As Francesco Cirillo said on his blog:

> *"Over 2 million people have already used the Pomodoro® Technique to transform their lives, making them more productive, more focused and even smarter."*

So, let's have a look at the main benefits of the Pomodoro technique through its effectiveness in the real world.

It motivates you to be productive

Kat Boogaard is a freelance writer and a self-proclaimed hater of productivity hacks. This is how she described herself:

> *"Admittedly, I've never been big on productivity hacks and tricks. Instead, I keep things pretty simple. I take a look at my planner (yes, a real paper planner—not my phone), jot down a list of things I want to get done that day, and then start hustling." [6]*

But after she kept hearing about the Pomodoro Techniques, she decided to give it a try. Even though she found working in small increments of time quite unnatural at the beginning, she decided to stick to it. Ultimately she found the technique to work really well for her:

> *"After some time, the technique started to really gel with me. I was focused and super productive during my work time, as I was eager to get as much completed during that 25-minute interval as I could. I didn't find myself mindlessly scrolling through Facebook or getting sucked in by those pesky clickbait articles. And as a notorious multitasker, I noticed that I was totally zoned in on the one project at hand." [6]*

As well as being easy to adopt, the Pomodoro Technique motivates you with an artificial deadline to get as much done as possible.

It gives units of value to your time

Alice Coleman is a co-founder of idearium, the company behind the Focus Booster app. The Pomodoro Technique is something that she regularly uses and occasionally mentions on her blog.

She wrote a blog post about the hidden benefits of the Pomodoro Technique. One benefit that she particularly emphasized was that the technique makes you value your time more. This is what she said about it:

> *"The pomodoro technique allows you to calculate the value of your time, plan your pomodoro sessions accordingly and then work to that plan to deliver a balanced outcome. Don't over deliver wasting time, and don't under-deliver because you didn't give yourself enough time." [7]*

To emphasize that the Pomodoro Technique is what she uses in her work, she has placed the following paragraph at the end of her article:

> *"Written in 10 pomodoro sessions, thank you for reading our view on why the pomodoro technique is effective."*

The Pomodoro Technique is a quick and easy way to record your time and add value to it.

It can be calming and refreshing

Another big proponent of the Pomodoro Technique is Sue Shellenbarger, a columnist for The Wall Street Journal. This is what she said about what she gained from practicing it:

> *"It eased my anxiety over the passing of time and also made me more efficient; refreshed by breaks, for example, I halved the total time required to fact-check a column." [8]*

It's still not for everyone

However, not everyone who has tried the Pomodoro Technique found it to be perfect. For example, Colin T. Miller, a software engineer, has tried the technique for a month. And these are the drawbacks of the technique he found:

> *"Pomodoros are an all or nothing affair. Either you work for 25 minutes straight to mark your X or you don't complete a pomodoro. Since marking that X is the measurable sign of progress, you start to shy away from engaging in an activity if it won't result in an X. For instance…meetings get in the way of pomodoros. Say I have a meeting set for 4:30pm. It is currently 4:10pm, meaning I only have 20 minutes between now and the meeting…In these instances I tend to not start*

a pomodoro because I won't have enough time to complete it anyway." [9]

So, even though the testimonies of Pomodoro are mostly positive, it might not be a solution that would suit everyone or every situation. To see how it's applicable to various activities that software developers are engaged in, I have tested the technique myself. And here is what I found.

My personal experience with Pomodoro

I have been practicing the Pomodoro Technique for some time and I found it to be exceptionally effective for certain types of work. However, there are also some categories of tasks that I wouldn't use Pomodoro for.

I found Pomodoro to be especially good while dealing with mundane routine tasks. These may include setting up a new Git repository, writing standard front-end templates, writing documentation, writing unit tests, reviewing somebody else's code, etc.

Before I started using Pomodoro, the work on these activities would drag for a fairly long time, even while applying the other techniques described in this book. For example, I would occasionally make pauses between the tasks or otherwise just do them slower than I would have been able to do otherwise.

But with Pomodoro, I can just squeeze as many of these tasks as possible into a productive round. I would do them at the best pace I'm capable of, so I am able to complete as many of them as possible.

And this ability to just get on with the work seems to be completely unconscious. I don't even have to deliberately think about the timer. There is something in the back of my mind that reminds me that the timer is running and there isn't that much time left.

I don't have any desire to do any clock-watching during the task. I know that the Pomodoro round isn't that long, so I am able to just focus on the task at hand and nothing else. In fact, I found the Pomodoro timer to be the most effective if I put the device it's running on out of my view. Usually, placing it behind the laptop I'm working on would suffice.

Same applies to reading technical documentation. Even if the technology itself is exciting, the documentation on how to use it will probably be very dry and boring. Before I was aware of the Pomodoro Technique, it used to take me a fairly long time to read a piece of technical documentation. I would occasionally pause and just distract myself with some more exciting activities, like checking my Facebook feed, or get bogged down in rereading particular sections.

Using the Pomodoro Technique, I no longer pause when I read the document. I just carry on for 25 minutes. And when the bell rings, I usually find that the break is long enough for me to digest the information. Then, when the new round starts, I can just carry on reading from where I left off. My reading became more focused, so I rarely have to re-read the sections I've read already.

Even though the break in between the rounds is technically a context switch and we have learned in chapter 2 that context switches are generally bad, I don't always find it to be a problem with Pomodoro. Firstly, when we finish the round, we take a break, so our mental energy gets restored instead of being drained by switching from one type of task to another. Secondly, we aren't making that many switches. And thirdly, a planned context switch is still better than a spontaneous context switch that you do purely because you feel a strong urge to distract yourself.

The other benefits of using Pomodoro are that I no longer feel guilty while taking a break, because all of those breaks are scheduled. Also, I don't feel as mentally drained at the end of the day as I used to before I knew what the Pomodoro Technique was.

But Pomodoro is not a tool that I use universally. For example, if my day is too fragmented by meetings, I may still use timers to complete certain tasks, but I would probably not adhere to the Pomodoro methodology. Also, there are certain types of tasks where I found the Pomodoro Technique to be somewhat counterproductive.

As a programmer, I do, on occasions, experience the state of flow. And I try to make the best use of it while it lasts. This means eliminating any potential distractions that can take me out of this state, including the timer and the list of microtasks. As soon as I feel that I am fully engaged in the task at hand, I just switch my timer off.

Also, it's inevitable that some of the tasks that software developers do require deep thinking. You might be solving some complex problem and have to hold a lot of variables in your head. If you distract yourself and take a break, this complex mental model that you hold in your head and worked so hard to build will disappear. And it will take time to rebuild it again. So, when faced with this type of task, I don't bother with Pomodoro.

This demonstrates that, even though the Pomodoro Technique is really good, it's not a Swiss army knife that can deal with any type of scenario. Sometimes you have to modify it to make it fit the situation better. Or sometimes it's not the right tool for the job at all.

Why Pomodoro is not one-size-fits-all

We have covered the brief history of the Pomodoro Technique, it's fundamental structure and the principles behind it. However, even though it's been designed to be suitable for many different scenarios, it's simply impossible that it will always be suitable everywhere and for everyone.

First of all, we are all different. Some of us are introverts, while others are extraverts. Some of us prefer to consume verbal information, while others are more comfortable with written communication. And the same applies to the way we work. What's the most optimal for one person may not be the best for someone else.

And the same applies to the Pomodoro Technique. For example, even though most people would probably find 25 minutes to be a reasonable duration of a productive round, for some people it will be unbearably long. But there would also be some people for whom it is ridiculously short.

Likewise, would you still have to force yourself to take a five minute break if you can't wait to get back to your task after only one minute of rest? What if you are the type of person that would completely lose interest in the task if you can't get started on it within the next minute or so? Believe me, I have actually met people like that!

What if you are naturally very efficient and focused and only occasionally need to apply productivity hacks? Why would you need to keep taking five minute breaks if you can just keep going non-stop the whole day long?

Also, even if the Pomodoro Technique is perfect for you, it may still not be the best tool for all situations, as I have personally discovered. Certain activities require long uninterrupted periods of deep work and Pomodoro timer will just cause unnecessary interruptions.

These hypothetical scenarios demonstrate that, despite its effectiveness, Pomodoro should not be treated as an automatic panacea. It's just a tool. And just like with any other tool, you can make adjustments to it as you see fit.

But even though the strict Pomodoro rules may not be suitable in a particular situation, this doesn't diminish the effectiveness of using timers. You may just need to do some trial and error to come up with a technique that suits you best.

How to develop your own technique of timing

The effectiveness of using timers when you work comes from the fact that they split your tasks into smaller chunks. So, if you set your timers for relatively short rounds, your brain will perceive the work ahead as small enough regardless of whether you stick to Pomodoro or not.

So, if the Pomodoro Technique doesn't happen to be a suitable solution, you can come up with your own technique. Or maybe you can even develop a number of different techniques and would use each in just a specific scenario.

Here are some examples of timer methods that you can try.

Adjust Pomodoro durations

The reason a Pomodoro round is 25 minutes is because it was assumed that this is the duration of time an average person would be able to maintain their focus for. Also, it's how long you can delay your response to calls or emails without upsetting people. This duration doesn't happen to be a magic number that was scientifically found to be the most optimal round for maximum productivity. So, if you find that this duration doesn't work well for you, you don't have to use it.

Same applies to the duration of the break. What if one minute is enough for you? Or maybe it's the other way round and you need at least 10 minutes?

Or maybe you'll find that keeping the durations constant throughout the day doesn't work for you. Perhaps at the beginning of the day you can have longer productive rounds and shorter breaks. But then, towards the end of the day, you will work at your best pace if you reduce the duration of the productive rounds and increase the duration of breaks.

Maybe you will even find that there are different rules that can be applied depending on how tired you are on any given day. We all sometimes miss out on a full night sleep and none of us would always feel fully rested while coming to work. Also, there might be circumstances beyond our control that would use up a lot of our mental energy even before we would start our day. For example, we may feel stressed because of an unusually bad traffic jam on the way to work.

And this is why the set of custom Pomodoro rules that worked well for you yesterday might not be applicable today. Maybe you will need shorter Pomodoros, longer breaks and fewer Pomodoros.

I cannot prescribe a personal customization of the Pomodoro rules to you, so you'll need to experiment if you dislike the original prescribed rules of the technique.

Do consecutive rounds with no break

This is a technique that I found to work fairly well for me. It's similar to Pomodoro, but you don't force yourself to take a break after the end of a productive round. You just instantly start the next round. And then the next. And you keep going until you feel reasonably tired.

It works in a similar way to going through the list of microtasks that we talked about in chapter 8. You can tell yourself that once the round is finished, you can stop. And then you can take as much time off as you need. But until the bell rings, you have to keep going.

And it has exactly the same effect on your brain as the list of microtasks. To you, nothing exists other than a short period of time that you have to fill with productive work. Even if the work is mundane or very hard, your brain will perceive it as manageable. After all, it will only have to work on the task for a little while. And then it can do something fun.

If it's only a short duration of time that you have to maintain your focus for, it becomes easy to fight the urge to procrastinate. You know exactly when your break will come if you'll want to take it, so it becomes easy to just hold off for a little while.

But then, once the bell rings, you can re-evaluate how you feel. If you feel like you can keep going, just go for another round. If you feel like having a break–have a break.

But to make this technique even more effective and build positive habits around it, you can introduce an additional rule. You cannot stop mid-round. If you start to feel like your attention starts to slip, wait until the end of the round to have your break. What I found is that the slip of attention may just be momentary anyway. Sometimes, I can get myself back in gear and just keep going for another round.

Perhaps, this method of using timers to maintain focus is not suitable for everyone. And it's much more exhausting than the bog-standard Pomodoro Technique. But one advantage the use of back-to-back rounds has over the Pomodoro Technique is that the former is much better at getting you into the state of flow. After all, this highly coveted mental state only happens when you do some challenging enough work for a continuous period of time. But the Pomodoro timer just interrupts it.

Set a one-off timer

This is another tool that I've used on occasions. It's about just having a single round of focused effort.

The best application of this is when you have almost finished for the day, but you only have one task ahead of you. Perhaps you realize that completing this task today will make tomorrow's workload a lot easier. Perhaps you want to complete it because you know that, if you don't, you will just be thinking about this task during the night and you won't be able to fall asleep until early morning.

But despite the huge benefits of completing this task today, there is only one problem. You are already tired after a busy day and you just can't get yourself in gear. Every time you try to make a start on this activity, you instinctively just open YouTube in your browser instead. You just have no more willpower left.

And this is precisely when a one-off timer comes into play. You set the timer and you tell yourself: "I just need to get done as much as I can during this round. And then I'm free to do whatever I want.".

And, more often than not, this action manages to convince your brain to squeeze out some additional mental resources to complete the task. You'll probably find that, once you get started, it's actually relatively easy to stick with it till the end. It's making a start that was hard. But you have managed to overcome this mental barrier by convincing your brain that there's only a little work that remains.

What to do when the bell rings is up to you. If you feel like carrying on, just carry on. But if you don't feel like doing any further work, then just stop. In any case, even if you haven't managed to complete the task, you still made a lot more progress on it than you would have done otherwise.

Bringing it all together

In this book, we've learned about various techniques on how to mold yourself into being as successful as you can possibly be in a software development career. But we didn't cover any technical skills specific to programming. All of the techniques described here are equally applicable to other careers and to things outside your work.

Even though various techniques described in this book are effective if used in isolation, they become the most effective when they are combined together, bringing all their benefits into play. When we consider the big picture of all the techniques we've covered, you'll see how they all complement each other and form a framework to alter your thoughts, behaviors and practices to achieve the best in your career that you can.

Using Pomodoro timers is an effective way to keep you focused on the task ahead. But your work will be even more efficient if you have pre-planned a list of microtasks (chapter 8). This way, you will not have to spend half of your Pomodoro round trying to figure out what to do. You will know exactly what to do by the time the round starts. The benefits of these two techniques compound when your microtask seems very achievable and the time you have to focus seems very manageable.

Knowing that the clock is ticking will help you to complete a bunch of mundane activities. But you'll probably derive more pleasure from the process if you apply Shisa Kanko during it (chapter 9). Also, this way, you won't just complete as many of these routine activities as possible, but you will also significantly minimize the chance of making accidental mistakes. Pointing and calling would get you embedded in the process.

But those are just the tactical techniques that you can apply during your work to make it easier, to keep from getting bored and to reduce errors. Of course they will make you effective, but what will make you even more effective is developing the right type of mindset for the job.

Also, you shouldn't forget that a programming career is not only about writing code. Even though the field often attracts introverts, you will have to deal with people to make any substantial progress in your career. At the very least, you need to gain trust and acquire a good reputation in the eyes of other people.

And this is where training your thoughts to align with a growth mindset comes in. The right kind of mindset will help you to motivate yourself to be the best you can be at what you do. But it will also help you to build core principles that will help you to become a person that everyone will want to work with.

One of the best ways to build the right type of mindset is to aggressively select the people you spend time with (chapter 4). You need to surround yourself with the types of people who would help you on your journey. And try your best not to associate with people that will hinder you.

Go to as many reputable software development conferences as possible. Join good programming forums online. And do your best to join a software company that enforces good standards.

One of the best ways of surrounding yourself with the right types of people while you spend time online is to tweak social media algorithms (chapter 5). Unfollow everyone who doesn't bring you value, refrain from interacting with distracting content and aggressively interact with as much helpful content as possible. This will let the algorithms know that this is the content you want, so you will start seeing more and more of it.

But to work on your growth mindset, interacting with helpful people is not enough. You also need to develop some internal convictions. A great place to start is to adopt the belief that everything is your responsibility unless proven otherwise (chapter 6). This way, you will become diligent and trustworthy.

But to work on your growth mindset, interacting with helpful people is not enough. You also need to develop some internal convictions. A great place to start is to adopt the belief that everything is your responsibility unless proven otherwise (chapter 6). This way, you will become diligent and trustworthy.

Another great way to develop the desire to succeed in your career is to treat it almost like a religion. You can apply similar principles at work to the ones that monks apply to life in the monastery (chapter 7).

But you also must be aware of those parts of the modern world that have been deliberately designed to fight for your attention. The algorithms behind social media platforms are perhaps the greatest obstacle to the formation of productive habits (chapter 1). So you need to be aware of what the most destructive parts of those algorithms are and minimize your exposure to them.

One of the fundamental habits that every successful programmer needs to master is the ability to do deep work (chapter 2). When you are solving complex problems, you will need to be able to maintain persistent focus for relatively long periods of time.

But all of these are built on the foundation of good habits (chapter 3). When you develop the right types of habits, your work will be easy. And so will be your career progress.

This brings us back in a circle. The concrete techniques that can be applied during your work, namely microtasks, Shisa Kanko and the use of timers, have all been designed to make hard work easy and to maximize your resistance to distractions. Therefore all of them are great for helping you to develop the right habits and mindset.

In this book, you have been given a toolbox. Now, it's up to you how you use it. I hope you'll find these tools as effective as I found them to be. And I hope that you have a fulfilling career as a programmer. But even if you decide that programming is not for you, you will still probably find this toolbox useful.

References

1. C. Northcote Parkinson - Parkinson's Law - The Economist - https://www.economist.com/news/1955/11/19/parkinsons-law
2. Cyril Northcote Parkinson - Parkinson's Law: Or The Pursuit Of Progress - Penguin Classics

3. Christian Jarrett - As new research findings shed light on the psychology of deadlines, we can learn ways that they can be used to increase focus and boost perseverance. - BBC Worklife - https://www.bbc.com/worklife/article/20200409-how-to-make-deadlines-motivating-not-stressful

4. Francesco Cirillo - The Pomodoro Technique - Lulu.com

5. Francesco Cirillo - The Pomodoro Technique - Francesco Cirillo Blog, https://francescocirillo.com/pages/pomodoro-technique

6. Kat Boogaard - Take It From Someone Who Hates Productivity Hacks—the Pomodoro Technique Actually Works - https://www.themuse.com/author/kat-boogaard

7. Alice Coleman - The hidden benefits of the pomodoro technique - https://www.focusboosterapp.com/blog/author/alice-coleman/

8. Sue Shellenbarger - No Time to Read This? Read This - The Wall Street Journal, https://www.wsj.com/articles/SB10001424052748704538404574541590534797908

9. Colin T. Miller - A Month of the Pomodoro Technique - https://developeraspirations.wordpress.com/2009/12/16/a-month-of-the-pomodoro-techniquethepositive/

Fiodar Sazanavets

Over time, you may forget some of the lessons from this book. This is normal, so to make sure that these lessons stay with you, you can download a brief summary of all the productivity hacks described in this book and more. It's available at: https://simpleprogrammer. com/10hacks/

Other books from Simple Programmer:

Soft Skills: The Software Developer's Life Manual, John Sonmez

Remote Work: Get a Job or Make a Career Working From Home, Will Gant

The Complete Software Developer's Career Guide, John Sonmez

www.ingramcontent.com/pod-product-compliance
Lightning Source LLC
LaVergne TN
LVHW081521050326
832903LV00025B/1578